WHEN YOUR DOG HAS CANCER

Making the Right Decisions for You and Your Dog

Lola Ball

Dogwise™ Publishing

Wenatchee, Washington U.S.A.

When Your Dog has Cancer
Making the Right Decisions for You and Your Dog
Lola Ball

Dogwise Publishing
A Division of Direct Book Service, Inc.
403 South Mission Street, Wenatchee, Washington 98801
1-509-663-9115, 1-800-776-2665
www.dogwisepublishing.com / info@dogwisepublishing.com

© 2013 Lola Ball
Cover photo: Irwin Dolobowsky
Interior photos: Julie Austin, Lola Ball, Carol Breeden, Lisa Cherian, Irwin Dolobowsky, Tombi Ericson, Barb Horsfall, David Lee, Dave and Katie Matison, Patty Olson, Carol Rowley, The Rowley Family, Sarah Vanston, Bruce Weber.
Graphic Design: Lindsay Peternell

Library of Congress Cataloging-in-Publication Data
Ball, Lola, 1969-
   When your dog has cancer : making the right decisions for you and your dog / by Lola Ball.
      pages cm
   Includes index.
   ISBN 978-1-61781-114-2
   1. Dogs--Diseases. 2. Cancer in animals. I. Title.
   SF992.C35B35 2013
   636.7'0896994--dc23
                                        2012041507

ISBN: 978-1-61781-114-2

Printed in the U.S.A.

IN MEMORY OF PORTER, MY BEST FRIEND

He is your friend, your partner,
your defender, your dog.
You are his life, his love, his leader.

He will be yours, faithful and
true, to the last beat of his heart.
You owe it to him to be worthy
of such devotion.

~ Unknown

TABLE OF CONTENTS

ACKNOWLEDGMENTS

I would like to thank the multitude of family, friends and acquaintances I met on the long path I took to write this book. First and foremost, I thank my Mom, who tirelessly fueled my love of animals by taking me to the Central Park Zoo and the Museum of Natural History in New York—over and over and over again. It is my pure love of animals and my desire to help other pet owners that are the impetus behind this book. Next, I would like to thank my wonderful son, Connor, who always supported me and was proud of me, even when he wasn't really sure what the end-product would look like.

During the writing of this book, I want to thank the following people who contributed to the review and editing of the book:

- Dr. Larry Siegler, for his encouragement and support of the book.

- Dr. Ella Bittel, for her tireless editing and review of the book, and her precise comments and direction.

- Dr. Lisa Reising, for her review and interest in the book.

- Mary Calanni, founder of the Big Mountain Wildlife Animal Sanctuary, for her approval and support of this book.

- The wonderful staff and editors at Dogwise Publishing, for their attention to detail and knowledge of book structure and design.

- Michelle Nichols, founder of the AHELP Project, who introduced me to the like-minded animal hospice community in the Seattle area.

- Dr. Jim Friedly, for his interest in the book.

- To Lisa Cherian and Irwin Dolobowsky, for the countless photo shoots with Scooby and me—you are both talented photographers and dear friends.

- My Mom, who reviewed and edited the book in its entirety and who never failed to give me the encouragement that I needed along the way.

In addition, I would like to thank the amazing people that I met (sometimes only over the phone) who shared their experiences with canine cancer and opened their hearts to me:

- Barb Horsfall and her story of Banner, the Golden Retriever.

- Carol Rowley and her story of Boomer, the Tibetan Terrier.

- Tombi Ericson and her story of Kess, the Border Collie flying disc dog extraordinaire.

- Jane Stanley and her story of Nelson Lake, the Australian Shepard/Border Collie mix with the million dollar smile.

- Michelle Nichols and her story of Sora, the European Boxer.

- Patty Olson and her story of Lewis, the Labrador Retriever/Border Collie mix.

- Carol Breeden and her story of Putter, the Bernese Mountain Dog.

- Dave and Katie Matison and their story of Alexsei, the Samoyed.

- David Lee and Jack, the Labrador Retriever/German Shepard mix.

- Sarah Vanston and Blake, the Rottweiler, German Shepard and Labrador Retriever mix.

- Dr. Luminita Sarbu, for her review of the oncology related sections of the book and her invaluable suggestions.

And perhaps most importantly, without whom this book would not have been possible, I want to recognize Porter, the most amazing Chocolate Labrador Retriever who ever lived, my first soulmate, and Jasper, the most amazing Yellow Labrador Retriever/Hound mix, my second soulmate, who both honored me with the privilege of caring for them through to the very end and who remained mine, faithful and true, to the last beats of their hearts. My only hope is that I was worthy of their devotion.

INTRODUCTION

You've just found out that your best friend has cancer, you're frightened and you're not quite sure where to go from here. That's where this step-by-step guide comes in to help you negotiate the medical decisions you'll be faced with and provides you practical information to approaching daily life with a dog with cancer. What you will find in this book is a guide to:

- Learning about your dog's diagnosis and what it really means, as well as the best way to get as many facts as you can up front.

- Understanding the types of cancer that your dog might contract and determining the stage and grade of the cancer once it is diagnosed.

- Evaluating options based on effectiveness, quality of life and cost, including hospice or palliative care, so that you and your dog, with support, can still enjoy a good quality of life. Learn how to easily compare each treatment option from the viewpoint of your dog.

- Creating a plan of action that is true to your dog and honors the trust you have in yourself.

- Triaging, or learning to prioritize, the basics of everyday life so that you can be prepared for a variety of situations and maintain a positive attitude.

- Addressing diet and nutrition to keep your dog strong by knowing what your dog should—and should not—be eating.

- Incorporating exercise and massage into your daily routine with your dog, which will also strengthen your bond with him through the power of touch.

- Understanding the natural dying process, so that you will be able to recognize where your dog is and honor his/her experience.

- Finding peace when the time comes and learning how to celebrate the life of your beloved dog.

Why I wrote this book

When my dog Porter was first diagnosed, I did not know anything about canine cancer. I found myself overwhelmed with the prospect of trying to choose the right course of treatment for a disease that I did not understand. Luckily, I had the benefit of a strong support system of family and friends who armed me with advice from their own personal experiences, as well as research that they performed on my behalf. Without a doubt, there was a lot I learned during our battle with cancer that came directly from books and my veterinarian. More importantly, perhaps, were the things I learned through trial and error that no book available at that time could teach me.

After Porter died from cancer, I decided to write a book to help others facing the same traumatic event. During my research, I realized the care I had provided to Porter was actually hospice care. I began to focus my research in that direction and participated in workshops and seminars to learn more about I could do for my dog at home myself, as well as the dying process in case I faced this situation again. I discovered that there is growing interest and momentum in hospice care for animals in this country, although many veterinarians have provided this type of care for their clients for years. In addition, I continued to speak to neighbors and friends to learn more about their personal struggles with their own dogs with cancer. I also learned that cancer strikes a surprisingly large number of dogs, so there are many people who could benefit from the experiences I have had and the knowledge I have gained.

When a second dog of mine was also diagnosed with cancer, I had the benefit of all the knowledge I gained from my research for this book. While the symptoms and progression of the disease, as well as my emotional ability to understand its course, were quite different from my first experience, a lot of what I had learned about hospice care remained the same and easily transferred to the care of Jasper, a beautiful yellow Labrador retriever/hound mix who I had adopted from a local animal sanctuary. To be honest, there were still times that I was so caught up in the moment of what was happening that I forgot what I had learned and made mistakes. So another important lesson I learned is that you need to be kind to yourself and accept that you are doing the best that you can in what is an emotionally difficult situation. It's very hard, after all, to entertain the thought that your beloved dog is in pain.

No matter how well equipped you become, it is important to recognize that every set of circumstances is different, every dog is different and we, as people and as pet owners, are different. A decision that makes sense for you may not make sense for someone else. It's important to proceed down a path that respects both you and your dog. While you don't want to make decisions too quickly, you don't want to waste time belaboring a course of action either.

In summary, I want to share everything I have discovered with you so that you are armed with the tools and resources you need to either help your dog win his/her battle with cancer or, if that is not possible due to an advanced stage of cancer, live out his/her days with a high quality of life. I firmly believe that this book will help you take on the role of caregiver for a dog with cancer and will give you the confidence to trust your instincts in gauging your dog's needs. No one knows your dog better than you, and no one is better equipped than you are to team with your dog.

Hospice care and advances in medical treatment

One of the things my research has taught me was that I could employ the concepts behind hospice and palliative care with my dogs once they contracted cancer. What does hospice and palliative care mean with respect to our animals? Many of us have personal experiences with hospice and/or palliative care for humans. Dame Cicely

Saunders is credited with the development of modern hospice principles in the 1950s, although hospice care has been evolving since the seventeenth century. By contrast, the concept of hospice and palliative care for our animals is very new and still evolving. According to the International Association of Animal Hospice and Palliative Care, "animal hospice is care for animals, focused on the patient's and family's needs; on living life as fully as possible until the time of death [with or without intervention]; and on attaining a degree of preparation for death." (Books and periodicals mentioned are listed in the Resources section.) While there are many established facilities around the world that provide hospice care for humans, there are few that provide animal hospice care. If you are interested in applying the principles of hospice care for your beloved animal at home, this book will help you understand how to navigate that path.

Similarly, while there is currently little "official" emphasis on animal hospice care today, I hope that this too will change in the future. Today, veterinary schools do not provide courses to students on hospice care; many individuals and organizations are working to change this, so perhaps we will see a shift to include hospice in veterinary curriculums in the future. In the list of resources that I provide at the end of the book, you will find links to many grassroots organizations that are trying to raise awareness of the virtues of hospice and palliative care for our pets. Hospice care has been used for humans for many years; it's high time that we expand this humane and loving care to our animal friends.

It is not easy to know whether hospice care is right for you and your dog. I had a very different perception of quality of life between the time I was first exposed to canine cancer and now. Initially, I mistakenly thought that if a dog was not eating or drinking or able to run and play, that this indicated that he wanted to, or was ready, to die. It was when I attended the *Spirits in Transition* seminar, created by Dr. Ella Bittel to teach animal lovers the art of hospice care, that I realized my experiences with Porter and Jasper showed they desired to live even at that stage of life. Simply because an animal is in some discomfort or suffering does not necessarily indicate that the animal wants to die. Dr. Bittel suggests that we consider that, just like many humans, animals may also want to live out their lives even if some level of discomfort is involved. And to provide comfort through the end of life is what hospice aims to do.

In Oregon and now also Washington, it is possible for terminally ill human patients to elect to take lethal medication to end their own lives. Dr. Helene Starks of the University of Washington has evaluated the 1998 to 2006 statistics relating to the Death with Dignity Act in the state of Oregon and found that the small number of patients who indeed took the medication to end their lives were neither in a rush to do it nor made the decision due to unbearable pain. In fact, once the underlying issues of many patients were identified and addressed, they no longer chose to end their lives. In 2007, less than sixteen in 10,000 terminally ill people in Oregon chose to take lethal medication, which means only 0.2% took the opportunity of end their lives prematurely.

When I learned this statistic, something clicked for me. I realized that my perception of what my dog might be feeling could be way off base and that, perhaps, I needed to pay even more attention to other physical indicators of happiness, such as tail wagging and degree of playfulness, as well as the strength of the human-canine bond. I realized that I needed to let go of my preconceived ideas of what a good quality of life might really mean.

This realization was an important factor in my ability to manage my second canine cancer experience much more gracefully than the first time. I now truly understood that indicators like the ability to drink, eat and run were perhaps not the key elements to a dog's happiness and will to live. In addition, as the body is slowly shutting down, some symptoms like lack of eating and drinking are merely the body's way of preparing itself for death. In the words of Bittel, "it appears most of our animals are very open to experience also the last part of their life, their own dying process. They don't bring the fear and resistance to it as many humans do." I think we have a tendency to forget that our animals live in the moment and are not caught up in the how's, where's and why's of dying.

Regardless of which method of care and treatment you choose, one thing you can be sure of is that advancements are continually being made in the treatment and prevention of canine cancer. As I was writing this book, the first drug to treat canine cancer was approved by the FDA in June, 2009. By the time you read this book, I hope that many more medicines and treatments are developed. Because the field of canine cancer research is growing so rapidly, I will arm you with a timeless approach to managing your dog's cancer and a set of reliable, trustworthy resources that you can reference to find out about the latest developments. I've included information on how to find out about current clinical trials and test treatment options. When you are evaluating your own situation, even five to ten years after the publish date of this book, you will still be able to glean valuable information to assist you and your dog on your canine cancer journey. There are even many free services available to you when you are faced with canine cancer, from blogs to bereavement hotlines to cancer prevention diets to animal massage videos.

How this book is organized

If this is your first experience dealing with canine cancer, the information you need to know about diagnoses, treatment and types of cancers are covered in the first three chapters. These chapters will enable you to get to an accurate diagnosis quickly, analyze options and chart a course of action for treatment. Chapter 4 covers hospice care in case your dog has terminal cancer. Chapters 5 and 6 focus on what you can do to improve your dog's life through diet and nutrition as well as massage, sleep and exercise. All of this can help you support your dog in his/her battle with cancer.

In Chapter 7, Prevention, I discuss the key steps that you can take to minimize your dog's exposure to environmental and nutritional factors that can contribute to cancer. While there is no guarantee that your dog won't develop cancer, at least you can have peace in the knowledge that you did your best to maximize your pet's journey towards good health and longevity. I didn't feel that this book would be complete without a discussion of prevention. While it may be too late to discuss prevention when you are in the throes of cancer, I think it is invaluable to know for any future animals who you bring into your life. While it may not seem likely when you are in the stages of grieving, many of us do eventually fall in love with another set of soulful eyes and teasing whiskers. And when we do, I think having all the right information up front is invaluable.

Chapter 8, The Natural Dying Process, is included to help you understand and be able to recognize the stages of the natural dying process, reach closure should your dog succumb to cancer, and encourage you to give some thought in advance as to how you would like to handle the body after your dog has passed on. Again, every animal is different and experiences will vary with respect to duration and exact characteristics, but it's important that you understand what to expect. My own experiences with the natural death of my beloved dogs were vastly different, both in terms of duration and the individual reactions of my dogs. As part of one of the workshops I attended, we watched a video that captured the natural dying process, which also showed it varied radically in duration and manifestation from dog to dog.

When you are faced with the end of life of your beloved pet, Chapter 9 spells out the stages of grief and lists resources that might be helpful in dealing with your sorrow and the loss of your animal companion. Many ways to memorialize your pet are discussed, including some very unusual suggestions that I have discovered over the years.

In Chapter 10, I will share the experiences of many friends and acquaintances that I have met on my journey to bring you this book, if only to impress upon you the varied nature of each of our canine cancer experiences. I will share my personal story as well, including the mistakes I made.

The final sections of the book provide a list of additional resources including books and websites that you may wish to review, as well as common medical terms that you may encounter.

CHAPTER 1
The Diagnosis

"Your dog has cancer." Words you never want to hear from a vet, of course, but may as is not an uncommon disease. After recovering from the shock, the first step on your journey to battle cancer is to evaluate the current condition of your dog and fully understand the facts surrounding the diagnosis you received.

Your veterinarian will most likely be your initial source for information. Ideally, this is someone who is familiar with your pet and his/her health history. Depending on your veterinarian's area of expertise, she may choose to refer you to a veterinary oncologist, a specialist who treats cancer. Such a specialist may be enlisted for a consultation or second opinion as she will be well-versed in standard cancer treatments and should have knowledge of experimental treatments or clinical trials that might be relevant to your dog. Depending on where you live, you can also try your local veterinary college.

An organization called Oncura Partners offers a *free* consultation to their customers. The consultation is online for veterinarians that have an account with Oncura. More information can be found on their website: www.oncurapartners.com. Pet owners should first ask their veterinarians if they have an account with Oncura, but if they do not, pet owners can call Oncura directly at 1-866-233-9100 to get referred to a veterinarian that does. Another option is Lap of Love, Veterinary Hospice and In-Home Euthanasia, www.lapoflove.com, which offers a fee service for families who have just received a cancer diagnosis (see Resources for contact information).

Tests to confirm a diagnosis of cancer

In most cases, either your vet or the specialist will want to conduct tests on your dog to reach a firm diagnosis if they suspect cancer. The following is a list of initial tests that may be prescribed:

- **Blood analysis.** A sample of your dog's blood will provide information regarding white and red blood cell counts, which can be an indication of whether your dog is fighting an infection. Note that a blood analysis alone will likely not provide a positive cancer diagnosis, but may be useful in evaluating the overall health and strength of your dog.

- **Urine analysis.** The presence or absence of bacteria, mineral crystals, blood and other compounds in the urine will help to complete a picture of your dog's overall health. As with blood analysis, urine analysis will likely not provide a positive cancer diagnosis, but may be useful in evaluating the overall health and strength of your dog.

- **X-rays.** An X-ray is a medical imaging technique that may show the presence of tumors or masses inside your dog. It provides a two dimensional (2-D) representation of your dog's internal organs and cavities. While X-rays can be extremely useful in identifying the presence of some tumors and other masses within your dog, they will likely not indicate whether a particular tumor or mass is benign or malignant, nor what type of cancer is present.

- **Ultrasound.** An ultrasound is another medical imaging technique that provides insight regarding what is happening internally within your dog; it also provides a 2-D representation of your dog's internal organs and cavities. Whereas an X-ray provides a static snapshot, ultrasound provides a more dynamic view, since the technician can position the ultrasound wand at different angles. Ultrasounds also reveal the presence or absence of blood flow which may help the doctor better diagnose a tumor or mass.

As with X-rays, ultrasound is extremely useful in locating and sizing tumors and masses within your dog, but likely cannot prove or disprove the malignancy of the tumor or mass. There are some cases, however, where an ultrasound can show malignancy if certain characteristics are exhibited on key organs. For example, with my second canine cancer experience, the ultrasound revealed metastatic lesions on the liver and spleen. This was a diagnosis of cancer, although the specific type of cancer could not be determined until a fine needle aspirate was taken and analyzed. Only then did I find out what kind of cancer it was.

- **Fine needle aspirate.** This is considered a minor surgical procedure that uses a very thin hollow needle to take samples from tumors or masses. These tissue samples from the tumor or mass can be identified as benign or malignant. Note that this method can result in false negatives or positives, as only a small sample of the total tissue is removed and malignant cells may be missed. In addition, if the mass is a fluid-filled cyst, there is a risk of rupture from the insertion of the needle. Similarly, there is the risk of hemorrhage, particularly if the tumor or mass is on an organ that is suspected to be cancerous.

NOTE: Be sure to ask the doctor performing the procedure to alert you if there are any risky aspirate sites before proceeding. You have the right to be notified of any potential risks prior to the procedure.

- **Biopsy.** This is a more invasive surgical procedure that is used to take larger tissue samples from tumors or masses suspected to be cancerous. As with the aspirate method discussed above, a sample of tissue taken from the tumor or mass can be identified as benign or malignant using this method. Because this method is a surgery, there are risks associated with anesthesia, infection, potential hemorrhages or ruptures. Lastly, depending on the location and nature of the tumor or mass, it may be a more effective approach to remove the mass entirely, with margins, rather than just sample it and potentially have to perform surgery a second time.

Depending on where the cancer is located, it might be necessary to test the functions of various organs to determine how well your dog may respond to surgery or other treatments. For example, if there is a tumor on one of your dog's kidneys, the veterinarian may prescribe a test to determine how well your dog might function with only one kidney. If the unaffected kidney is strong enough, then removing the kidney with the tumor may present a solid option to treat the cancer. However, if your dog's kidney strength is poor, this would not be a good option.

Reviewing the tests

Once you have the results of these tests, you will be given either a firm diagnosis of a specific type of cancer and its location, or at least a narrowed down list of possibilities. Having a complete picture of your dog's diagnosis should help you, your vet and any specialists who have been consulted to begin to create a treatment plan (covered in more detail in Chapter 3) to suit your dog's particular needs. I would recommend that you either bring someone with you to the vet's office when you receive the diagnosis or take careful notes. It's difficult to remember details when a diagnosis of cancer is made, especially if you are as stressed as you likely will be. It's also important to arm yourself with a list of questions to ask so that you don't forget anything.

To the extent possible, I recommend that you get as many tests as necessary performed (the less invasive, the better) so that you can learn more about the type of cancer that you are dealing with. Based on the type of cancer and how far it has spread, you will have a better understanding of what your options for treatment are. Be prepared, however, for incomplete answers as was the case with my canine cancer experiences and others described in this book.

The hardest part of this process is when there is no clear cut answer in determining how best to treat your dog, even once all the test results have come back. For example, when I learned that my first dog had cancer and that the next step was an ultrasound, I was sure that once I had the ultrasound results, I would know what kind of cancer he had and what I would need to do about it. I knew that if I had the facts, I wouldn't be worried about what to do since I would know what I was dealing with. I felt confident that I could do the research and weigh the risks, and the "right" thing to do would be obvious. What I didn't count on was the fact that the tests were not as conclusive as I would have preferred. In fact, when I was presented with the results, I found them to be somewhat confusing and I didn't have a very clear sense of what the "right" thing to do was at all. Be prepared for this. Sometimes science and medicine are more of an "art" than perhaps we'd like them to be.

> During my first canine cancer experience, even once the ultrasound and fine needle aspirates were performed, I still didn't have a clear, complete picture of the situation. What I did know was that he had hemangiosarcoma, at the least, although it wasn't entirely clear how many tumors were cancerous and how many were benign. Of the five tumors he had, only three were candidates for a fine needle aspirate. The other two were in tissue areas that were deemed risky for aspirates — the risk being that they would bleed and cause hemorrhaging. Of the three tumors that were aspirated, one was benign. One showed only blood cells, which did not indicate the presence or absence of cancer. The final tumor was the one that showed cells that were indicative of hemangiosarcoma. Based on this information, and the fact that there were so many tumors, the most reasonable conclusion was that the cancer had metastasized.

Begin to assemble a team

Once you have received a firm diagnosis, I would recommend assembling a cancer treatment team of veterinarians and animal caregivers. For example, if your family veterinarian practices Western medicine, I would encourage you to seek out the opinion of a holistic or naturopathic veterinarian as well. A holistic vet may either offer alternate treatment options to combat the cancer or suggest ways to reduce the degree of pain and complications that your dog may experience through the use of alternative therapies such as acupuncture, Chinese medicine and homeopathy. Similarly, if your veterinarian specializes in alternative medicine, homeopathy, Chinese medicine or holistic care, I would also encourage you to solicit the opinion of both general and specialized veterinarians such as veterinary oncologists who are well versed in Western practices. They will likely be most knowledgeable regarding recent advances in treatments for canine cancers. Each discipline of medicine has its value and can be combined in a complementary manner. Your budget obviously will dictate the number of professionals you can use in your plan. See the final section of the book for resources to assist you in finding a reputable veterinarian.

It is important to ask your practitioners lots of questions to assess not only their confidence in the diagnosis of cancer, but also their experience with the treatments that they are recommending to you. You can also ask your veterinarian to recommend others within their own practice or specialists who are either dealing with a similar diagnosis or have in the past. This is the time to engage family and friends who might have had dogs with cancer and who can offer you not only emotional support, but also the wisdom of their own experiences. See Chapter 10 for a few real-life examples of the range of possible experiences with canine cancer.

CHAPTER 2
Types of Cancer

The purpose of this chapter is not to provide a detailed analysis of all the types cancer a dog might possibly contract. There are many great books on the market that cover this material, written by veterinarians and others with extensive medical training. I have included several in the Resources section for those who want to do more research. Instead, the purpose of this chapter is to describe the most common kinds of cancer that are prevalent in dogs, ones you may encounter if your dog does indeed have cancer.

Generally speaking, the worst types of cancers are hemangiosarcomas or osteosarcomas, as these types have a tendency to be more aggressive or are discovered at more advanced stages. Therefore treatment options may be limited depending on the location and quantity of the tumors. If the cancer is present in more than one area of the body, it is likely that the cancer has metastasized. This means that the cancer is aggressively and actively growing. It is more difficult to treat cancer successfully if it has progressed to this stage. One of the more successfully treatable forms of cancer is lymphoma, as it typically responds to traditional treatment methods more readily than some of the other types. That said, there are exceptions to every rule.

> *With my second canine cancer experience, by the time I knew anything was wrong, my dog had metastatic lesions on his liver and spleen, which is not a typical representation*

of the mast cell tumor cancer he had. Remember that regardless of what we know about various types of cancer and how they manifest, there are exceptions to every rule.

Common types of canine cancer

Hemangiosarcoma. This is a cancer that occurs in areas where there are many blood vessels, for example, organs like the spleen and pancreas, or in the abdominal region. It often metastasizes to the liver.

Osteosarcomas. This is a cancer of the bone. It tends to appear on the long bones of the legs or the flat bones of the ribs, particularly in middle-aged dogs. It is more common in males than females and in larger breeds.

Testicular cancer. Cancer of the testes and, as such, affects only male dogs. Dogs that are neutered do not contract this type of cancer.

Mammary cancer. Cancer that affects the mammary glands in female dogs. Bitches who are spayed are less likely to develop this type of cancer. Just as with humans, it is possible for a male dog to have this type of cancer, but this happens infrequently. About half of mammary tumors are malignant. They may spread, especially to the lungs.

Melanoma. Skin and/or mouth cancer.

Mast cell tumor or "mastocytoma." This is a type of cancer most commonly found on the skin, but can also occur in the respiratory system (such as the lungs or the nose) or in the digestive tract (such as the stomach or intestines). It is the most common form of skin tumor in dogs, but can manifest itself in a variety of ways. I recommend that any skin tumors or growths be removed from your dog be tested for cancer. If cancer cells are present, but not entirely removed, the cancer can grow and spread to other parts of the body unchecked. The most challenging aspect of the mast cells is that they have the potential to release large amounts of chemicals naturally found in the body such as histamine, heparin, proteolytic enzymes, etc. without any warning. This can cause what is known as a degranulation event. During a degranulation event, the dog's body is overwhelmed with this influx of chemicals, which can result in vomiting, internal bleeding, nausea, decreased appetite and even death. If your dog has this type of cancer, you must monitor him very carefully and bring him to an emergency clinic immediately if he becomes very lethargic or collapses.

> My second canine cancer experience was with mast cell tumor cancer, and I was surprised that my veterinarian prescribed such over-the-counter drugs as Pepcid AC, an acid reducer, and Sudafed, an antihistamine. This made sense once I learned that these were prescribed to combat the effects of the degranulation events (see mast cell tumor section above) that my dog was experiencing. It also explained his intense nausea, which was treated with a prescription for Cerenia, an anti-nausea drug made especially for dogs. This made it possible for him to eat his daily meals. I also learned that prednisone, a steroid that is commonly used as part of most chemotherapy treatments, is also often prescribed for dogs with mast cell tumors. This is because prednisone will actually help to shrink the size of the tumors and provide some relief of the common symptoms I described, as well as increase energy and appetite. Be warned that prednisone also has side effects of increased thirst and urination, which can lead to incontinence. In addition, about 5% of dogs do not respond well to prednisone and experience worsened health. This was the case with my dog, who could hardly move after his first dose of prednisone. I stopped using it immediately. Whenever administering any new medication to your dog, keep a sharp watch for the first 24 hours so that you can monitor any adverse reactions and take appropriate action. That said, you should continue to monitor your dog's behavior and response to medication over time as well. Keeping a daily journal and documenting what your dog eats and drinks, as well as how he behaves, will help you to identify trends over time.

Lymphosarcoma (lymphoma). Lymph node cancer can occur wherever there are lymph nodes in the body. It is the most common type of cancer in dogs and also the most treatable, particularly if found early on. Remission is possible, often after chemotherapy treatment, but each subsequent remission is shorter. The average survival rate is only four to six weeks with no treatment, and six to eleven months with chemotherapy. One of the interviews in Chapter 10 of this book contains a pet owner's experience with canine lymphoma, where the dog has been in remission for over two years.

Cancer location, grading and staging

As in humans, cancer can occur almost anywhere in a dog's body. Tumors can be located in many parts of the body including the brain, bladder, lungs, abdomen, spleen, stomach, pancreas, kidney, skin, lymph nodes, bone and blood. If your dog is diagnosed with a cancer, it is critical that you understand the type of cancer and learn what you can about its characteristics.

Tumors can be both graded and staged to indicate how severe the condition is. Grading defines how aggressive a malignant tumor is. (If the cancer has metastasized, or begun to spread to other parts of the body beyond the initial site of the tumor, then the grade is irrelevant.) Staging, typically expressed on a scale of one to four, indicates how much it has spread throughout the body. The higher the number, the more likely the tumor is more advanced or aggressive, or that it has metastasized. In the case of benign tumors, your veterinarian may or may not advise surgery or other action, such as supplements or Chinese herbs. Some benign tumors may have a propensity to become malignant so, as with all decisions, you must weigh your situation individually.

Recognizing the signs

Cancer in general, whether in humans or dogs, is best caught in the early stages when it is more easily treatable and before it is allowed to spread to other organs. You may be able to save your dog's life in a situation that otherwise would have been terminal by knowing what to look for and keeping tabs on your dog's condition. It is a good idea to perform regular hands-on checks for growths or any abnormalities over your dog's body, including ears, eyes, nose, mouth, legs and tail. I regularly feel every inch of my dogs' bodies, so that I can easily recognize a new lump, skin tag or changes in existing lumps. To be honest, it is a good practice to perform this check on your own body as well; why not monitor your dog at the same time, so that you can catch changes or abnormalities sooner, rather than later? Cancer is definitely a case where the old adage, "an ounce of prevention is worth a pound of cure," rings true. Chapter 7 contains a list of simple, no-nonsense ways in which you can make a best effort in preventing your dog from ever having cancer in the first place.

That said, what you need to be cognizant of are things that are out of the ordinary or non-characteristic for your dog. If your dog has always had a healthy appetite, and then suddenly loses interest in food, that is a warning sign. Or, if your dog has always been eager to take a walk, but lately would rather take a nap, this is another potential sign that something is awry. There are also physical differences that you should monitor, such as differences in the appearance of urine and stools. Has the color of urine changed to orange or red? Does blood appear in stools or are stools consistently malformed and runny, i.e., diarrhea, for significant periods of time? Is there an area of the body that is enlarged or not healing properly? Does your dog have a growth that seems to be increasing in size rapidly? While this is not a guarantee that a growth is cancerous, any fast growth should be investigated.

With my first dog who had cancer, the initial indication that anything was wrong was the red tinge I saw in his urine. By that time, however, the cancer had already metastasized. In the case of my second dog with cancer, the first unusual symptom he exhibited was vomiting after every meal. Since I did not know what was causing this until the ultrasound results were available, my veterinarian suspected that he was nauseous and he was given anti-nausea medicine (Cerenia). With that medication he was able to eat normally again, at least for a short while. After a few days, he stopped wanting to eat altogether. As you read through the personal stories in Chapter 10, you'll see that the initial symptoms ranged as follows:

- Wounds that would not heal and associated lameness.
- Persistent coughing.
- Unusual growths or unexplained skin conditions.
- Sudden appearance of seizures.
- Sudden blindness.

- Appearance of blood in urine.

- Vomiting and lack of appetite.

- Pain during normal everyday activities, like jumping or running.

- Sensitivity during physical examination, i.e., rectal thermometer.

In summary

Ensure you understand the following key points, as these will be most helpful to you in understanding your dog's diagnosis:

- Cancer type.

- Stage and grade of cancer.

- Location of cancer.

- Metastasis determination.

- General prognosis.

Chapter 3

Treatment Plans

One of the most overwhelming things about canine cancer is that each type has different treatment options, and that the prognosis will be varied based on factors such as the age and health of your dog in addition to the stage of the cancer. Depending on how aggressive the particular cancer is in your dog, the possible treatment and prognosis may differ. This only complicates matters even more.

Coming up with the proper treatment plan for your dog involves two equally important elements. The first focuses on the physical aspects of your dog's condition and the medical alternatives available to treat his cancer. The second revolves around you as the dog's owner. How much time, effort and money can you put into caring for your dog? These factors in turn can be influenced by things as wide ranging as your personal philosophies, ability to handle stress and views on quality of life. Recognize that in terms of your role as owner, there is no right or wrong answer. But you must ask yourself a number of questions in order to be content with the treatment plan you choose. The first part of this chapter will focus on medical treatments and the second part will focus on how you decide to proceed based on your philosophy, wants and needs.

Questions to ask

As you are progressing through appointments with your dog's primary veterinarian and other specialists, you need to gather answers to the following questions in order to begin to have confidence in any given treatment plan:

- What kind of cancer does your dog have?
- What is the location of the tumor(s)?
- What is the stage and grade of the tumor(s)?
- What is the typical progression of this type of cancer and how will the progression of the disease manifest itself?
- What are the associated risk factors of the recommended treatment?
- How much will the recommended treatment cost?
- What is the historical success rate of the recommended treatment?
- What is the state of your dog's current health?
- What is his/her health history, including previous and current illnesses?
- Given your dog's health history, age and other factors, what is the likely success rate of this treatment?
- What is your dog's experience with previous surgeries? Does your dog handle anesthesia well? How has he responded to surgery in the past?

Overview of treatments used to fight cancer

In this section, the more commonly prescribed medical treatments are presented to give you an overview of what they involve.

Surgery

Surgical procedures are often recommended for the removal of the tumor(s). It requires that your dog be put under anesthesia, shaved and stitched/stapled. Depending on where the stitches are, you will likely need to use a cone over his head so that he cannot reach the stitches. (If your dogs are anything like mine, they don't like this. There are some better cone designs available today, called "soft cone e-collars." Many use Velcro closures and allow you to thread your dog's own collar to secure it. See the Resources section for some vendors who supply these more comfortable cones.) Assuming that your dog is healthy enough to endure the surgery and that the tumor can be safely removed via this method, this is by far the best way to remove the cancer. Be sure to request that sufficient margins around the tumor or mass be removed as well. Kess, one of the dogs whose story is profiled in the final chapter of the book, had a rare form of cancer called synovial cell sarcoma in her right hind leg. The best course of action for this type of cancer is to surgically remove the affected limb. It has been over a year since her surgery, and Kess has not only been cancer-free, but is also a champion three-legged flying disc dog.

If your dog will have any surgery to remove a tumor or mass, you will hear the terms, "margins" or "with margins," used frequently. What this means is that, in addition to the tumor or mass itself, the surgeon will also remove some of the tissue around the tumor or mass, to ensure that the entire tumor or mass is removed. The last thing you want is to have some residual, potentially cancerous, tissue remain that may require additional surgery later. It's better to take out a little extra tissue on the first try than to risk the whole procedure again.

Any surgery carries the potential risk of infection and complications. It's best to limit the number of surgeries. You might be faced with the case where surgery may not remove a tumor in its entirety. Or perhaps, there might be so many tumors that it would require multiple surgeries to remove them all. In these circumstances surgery may not be worth the risk.

Chemotherapy

Chemotherapy involves the use any one of a variety of drugs (carboplatin, cisplatin, chlorambucil, doxorubicin, prednisone, etc.) to attack and destroy cancer cells. Often, these drugs are used in combination with each other. There are several reasons that this approach is taken according to veterinarian Dr. Shawn Messonnier, whose many books are listed in the Resources. Since cancer cells are in various stages of growth at any given time, and because each drug affects a different cycle of growth, using a variety of drugs at one time will be more effective in killing the greatest number of cancer cells compared to simply using one drug that affects only one stage of growth. The increased effectiveness of combinations of drugs means that smaller doses of each drug may be used; this has the additional benefit of minimizing side effects, some of which are toxic. It has also been found that this treatment approach may reduce the chances of the cells becoming resistant to specific drugs. In her book *Help Your Dog Fight Cancer*, Laurie Kaplan has compiled a table that describes common chemotherapy drugs and their side effects. This table is a good starting point if you are seriously considering chemotherapy as a treatment option.

Radiation therapy

Similar to an X-ray but used in higher doses, radiation therapy can be targeted to kill cells that are undergoing rapid growth, which is the case with cancer cells. There are three main types of radiation according to Messonnier: external beam radiation; internal radiation; and palliative radiation. External beam radiation releases high-energy beams and does not result in pain after treatment. Less common is internal radiation, which delivers short-range radiation by special tubes, seeds, implants or special chemicals called radiochemicals specifically designed for this purpose. A specific type of internal radiation is called brachytherapy. It uses radioactive beads that are surgically implanted into a tumor. Because brachytherapy targets the tumor directly, fewer overall treatments are required than with traditional radiation techniques. At Kansas State University, doctors have found this treatment to be a good approach when surgical removal of the entire tumor is not an option. The goal of palliative radiation is to make pets more comfortable by shrinking tumors, slowing tumor growth and relieving pain in situations where the cancer is not curable.

> *Radiation treatments are typically performed outside of normal business hours in human hospitals, and dog patients need to be anaesthetized at each visit. Treatments for an aggressive cancer, for instance, might require three visits per week. Remember this when considering these treatments.*

Immunotherapy/Genetic immunotherapy

Immunotherapy can be used to prevent or treat existing cancers. This technique tries to stimulate the body's immune system to heal itself and attack the cancer cells. The genes used are either modified canine genes or can also be non-canine genes; the goal is to trigger a stronger response from the dog's own immune system. Cancer vaccines are an example of this method. The first canine cancer vaccine created was for canine oral melanoma, and it was intended for use after the tumor had first been treated with surgery and/or radiation. The chart below shows the increased survival time that has thus far been experienced with the use of the vaccine based on research led by Dr. P.J. Bergman.

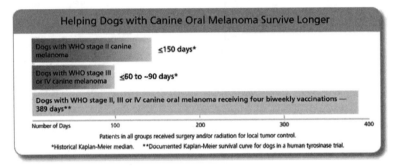

These results are certainly very impressive. As research continues in this field, perhaps more canine cancer vaccines will be available.

Photodynamic therapy

This technique uses a special drug that is known as a photosensitizer that targets cancer cells. Once the drug is concentrated in the cancer cells, a specific wavelength of light is used to activate the photosensitizer drug and release a special type of oxygen that kills the cancer cells. This treatment method can be effective in cases of canine prostate cancer.

Antiangiogenic therapy

Antiangiogenic therapy uses special drugs to prevent cancer cells from receiving a supply of blood, the source of oxygen and nutrients for the cancer cells. Tumors rely on the creation of new blood vessels as they grow. One of these drugs is called Palladia and is used to treat skin-based mast cell tumors. It works in two ways, by killing tumor cells and by cutting off the blood supply to tumors. "This cancer drug approval for dogs is an important step forward for veterinary medicine," says Dr. Bernadette Dunham, director of FDA's Center for Veterinary Medicine. "Prior to this approval, veterinarians had to rely on human oncology drugs, without knowledge of how safe or effective they would be for dogs. Today's approval offers dog owners, in consultation with their veterinarian, an option for treatment of their dog's cancer."

Cryosurgery

Cryosurgery is used to treat surface tumors (skin, etc.) which can be frozen using liquid nitrogen in the same way warts are sometimes treated in humans. This method does not require anesthesia and is relatively inexpensive. Tumors that are on the surface of the skin or in the mouth are the best candidates for this method. Since only specialized clinics have this type of equipment, it will likely be necessary to find a veterinary oncologist.

Hyperthermia or thermal therapy

This is the opposite of the cryosurgery. Instead of freezing, very high levels of heat are applied to the tumors with the intent of killing the cancerous cells. Heat can be applied via microwave, radiofrequency or ultrasound techniques.

Traditional Chinese medicine

This type of treatment typically includes Chinese herbal medicine and/or acupuncture. A variety of Chinese herbs are used to slow the growth of tumors, reduce the size of tumors and enhance the immune system. Acupuncture can be useful to relieve and/or reduce any pain caused by the cancer and improve the immune system.

Supplemental treatments

These include herbal supplements, homeopathy and energy medicine. I know several people who have had success treating cancer with herbal medicines, such as Essiac and mushrooms. More details on these supplements can be found in Chapter 5. There are also spiritual and alternative options that include prayer, positive thinking, energy work, etc. I encourage you to be open to all alternatives.

A comparison of treatment options

Let's take a comparative look at each of these methods and some of the pros and cons:

Treatment Method	Pros	Cons
Surgery	Good chance at removing cancer in its entirety, if sufficient margins are removed.	Invasive and traumatic for your dog; possibly traumatic for you. May not be an option depending on where the cancer is located (pancreas, etc.). Cost. Risk of infection and other complications. Limited movement post-op. Cone may be required. Recovery time may be slow.

Treatment Method	Pros	Cons
Chemotherapy	Can shrink tumors. Can slow down cancer growth. Commonly used against lymphoma successfully.	Traumatic for your dog, and potentially for you. Immune system becomes suppressed, increasing chances for other infections. Has not been shown to cure cancer. Cannot predict/ ensure length of time that life will be extended. Cost and time. Does not work well for all cancer types, such as hemangio-sarcoma. Subsequent remis-sion periods are reduced with repeat chemotherapy. Possible gastro-intestinal upset (vomiting, diarrhea, nausea).

Treatment Method	Pros	Cons
Radiation therapy	Can shrink tumors. Can slow down cancer growth. Can reduce pain. A method called low-dose rate irradiation has found promise in treating lymphoma. Specialized forms of internal radiation may require fewer treatments than traditional radiation therapy because of their targeted approach.	Potential exposure of healthy cells to high amounts of radiation. Localized burn, like sunburn, and loss of hair in treatment area. Fatigue and loss of appetite. May be difficult to find a local facility that performs specialized forms of internal radiation.
Immunotherapy/ Genetic immunotherapy	Can be quite effective in extending your dog's lifespan. Available for oral melanoma.	Not as commonly obtained as other methods of treatment. Cost. May require tumor to be removed first. Not available for every type of cancer.

Treatment Method	Pros	Cons
Photodynamic therapy	Can be effective in canine prostate cancer.	Not as commonly obtained as other methods of treatment.

Cost. |
| Antiangiogenic therapy | Tumor cells not likely to become resistant to this form of treatment.

Relatively nontoxic

Causes fewer side effects than traditional chemotherapy. | Not as commonly obtained as other methods of treatment.

Cost.

Not available for every cancer type. |
| Cryosurgery | Works well for surface tumors.

Not as invasive as traditional surgery.

Shorter recovery than traditional surgery. | Internal tumors cannot be treated this way. |
| Hyperthermia | When used in conjunction with chemotherapy and radiation, dogs may have higher rates of remission and survival. | A high enough level of heat must be reached for this method to be effective.

Not readily available. |

Treatment Method	Pros	Cons
Acupuncture and Chinese Herbs	Acupuncture is a highly effective way to treat pain. Lower cost than most of these other treatments.	Chinese herbs do not have a good taste and so are difficult to feed to a dog with a finicky appetite. Depending on stage of cancer, could be too late, but could still be used as palliative therapy.

Once you know what kind of cancer you are (likely) dealing with, you can use the table above to help guide your decision for which treatment type might work best for you and your dog. The most commonly offered forms of treatment are surgery, chemotherapy, and radiation. However, these forms of treatment will not necessarily "cure" your pet. According to Dr. R. M. Clemmons at the University of Florida, "on average, the success of Western approaches to cancer provides 1 to 18 months of relief from the cancer. While longer survival times are seen with certain forms of cancer, the long term prognosis for even the best forms of systemic cancer is poor to grave."

It would be ideal if only complementary and non-invasive treatments could be used to treat all cancers successfully. Barring that option, perhaps the "best" type of cancer to have is one where the entire cancerous area can be safely removed via surgery. But in many cases, and as was the case in my canine cancer experiences, surgery may not be an option due to the location and number of tumors. I think of chemotherapy as a good course to take if the cancer is detected early enough and it is directed toward a minimal number of tumors that are small in size. If not, the likelihood of a "cure" is minimal. According to Dr. Messonnier, it's important to note in considering a course of treatment for your dog that "in most cases, veterinarians don't cure cancer in pets but rather help them live longer by putting the cancer into remission for as long as possible. A main reason for this is that we use lower, less toxic doses of chemotherapy than are used in people. This is done specifically to minimize side effects; few pet owners would opt for chemotherapy if their pets experienced the same side effects commonly seen in people. The trade-off is that chemotherapy usually doesn't kill all the cancer cells, and remissions don't last as long in pets as in people." As with remission in humans, each subsequent remission period is shorter.

If your veterinarian offers you more than one treatment option, you will need to find a way to evaluate and compare these options. Some people may find it helpful to view the pros and cons of their options in a more visual representation, so feel free to create a table or diagram, if that works for you. What follows is a list of factors to consider when performing this comparison:

- **% Tumor Removal.** Will the treatment remove all of the cancer, or will some of it remain?

- **% Tumor Reduction.** Is the treatment effective in reducing the size of the tumor(s), or perhaps slowing its growth?

- **Estimated Treatment Effectiveness.** How likely is it that the treatment will achieve the expected result? Are there risks?

- **Post-Treatment Cons.** Are there any negative effects from the treatment that you should be aware of such as limited mobility?

- **Survival Rate, Pre-Treatment.** If your dog were not to receive any treatment, what would his expected survival rate be?

- **Survival Rate, Post-Treatment.** What is the expected survival rate after the treatment?

- **Degree of Pain/Discomfort, Pre-Treatment.** Prior to the treatment, how much pain or discomfort is your dog experiencing?

- **Degree of Pain/Discomfort, Post-Treatment.** Will the amount of pain or discomfort diminish or increase after treatment?

- **Quality of Life, Pre-Treatment.** What is your dog's quality of life currently? Is he able to do all of his normal daily activities?

- **Quality of Life, Post-Treatment.** How will your dog's quality of life change after treatment? Will it improve or worsen?

- **Treatment Risks.** Are there any risks of the treatment that need to be considered? Are there side effects that you should be aware of?

- **Treatment Cost.** Last, but not least, how much does the treatment cost? Can you comfortably afford it? For example, chemotherapy generally costs $3000 to $4000 for cases of lymphoma, but this cost can go up if there are complications.

Once you identified the key differences between your available options, it will be easier to compare the benefits of each.

Ongoing research and clinical trials

There are several organizations that are involved in canine cancer research and run clinical trials that you may be able to participate in. It may be worthwhile to visit these websites to learn about new cancer treatment options, prior to making your final decision. A few of these sites are as follows:

- Animal Cancer Treatment Program, School of Veterinary Medicine, University of Wisconsin – Madison: http://www. vetmed.wisc.edu/Animal_Cancer_Treatment.9.3.html

  A list of their current trials can be found here: http:// uwveterinarycare.wisc. edu/rdvm/trials.htm

- Canine Health Foundation, American Kennel Club, http:// www.akcchf.org/

  A list of their active grants can be found here: http://www. akcchf. org/research/grants/funded-grants/

- Morris Animal Foundation of Colorado, http://www.cure-caninecancer.org/

  Search for active, dog, cancer studies here: http://www. morrisanimalfoundation. org/our-research/studies.html

- List of Veterinary Teaching Hospitals, http://landofpuregold. com/cancer/vet.htm

  A list of current clinical trials can be found here: http://cancer. landofpuregold.com/trials.htm. This site listed eighteen organizations that were conducting clinical trials at the time of the writing of this book.

How to make decisions about treatment options

Now that you have learned as much as you can about all of the possible medical treatments and their pros and cons, you must decide how you want to proceed. No matter what the veterinarians and specialists recommend, the decision, as the dog's owner, is yours. Certainly you will want to consider all options and listen to the recommendations of the professionals. But ultimately you will need to make the decisions and be able to trust your own judgment and instincts.

My recommendation is you ask yourself the following questions, keeping in mind that there is no right or wrong answer:

- How does your dog's illness affect you? Are you going to be able to handle the stress of seeing your dog struggle against the disease? Can you tolerate seeing your dog in pain?

- Are you or your family/friends/neighbors going to be able to devote the time to care for your dog at home? If not, can you afford to hire someone to care for your dog if need be?

- Are you capable of providing your dog certain types of medical assistance, such as giving your dog pills and medicine?

- Can you afford surgery and the longer term medical expenses of your dog's treatments?

- Do you know what quality of life your dog needs to able to have in order for you to keep treatments going? Some factors to consider might be:
  - Can your dog still walk on his own?
  - Can your dog still eat and drink on his own?
  - Can your dog still play with toys?

    o   Can your dog tolerate being handled and touched?

    o   Can your dog relieve himself on his own?

Another way to help yourself decide on the proper course of action for your dog is to think about what the possible outcomes of any given treatment might be. Dr. Richard Pitcairn suggests that there are three possible outcomes with each treatment:

1. Help maintain a good-quality life during the time re-maining. Generally this involves minimizing pain in cases that are terminal.

2. Extend life beyond what would occur if no treatment is given. Here the focus is on maximizing the dog's lifes-pan.

3. Cure the condition with diminution or disappearance of the tumors. This outcome applies when the disease can be cured.

You need to ask yourself which of these outcomes is possible for your dog and then go back to the questions above and determine if you have the emotional and financial wherewithal to pursue them, assuming that you are satisfied with what you expect the dog's qual-ity of life to be in each case. At the end of the day, I think we can all agree on the following goals:

• Minimization of any pain for our animals.

• Maximization of their quality of life

• And, if not in conflict with these first two goals, a third goal could be the maximization of lifespan.

If we can think about treatment and outcomes with respect to these goals, the comparison factors on pages 26 to 30 can help to under-stand how best to achieve these goals.

Take some time for self-reflection

As mentioned above, there is no right or wrong answer when it comes to choosing a treatment option for cancer. In fact, even go-ing through the process of gaining knowledge and looking at your own wants and needs may not work. You may just need to look into the eyes of your best friend and see what he tells you. Our dogs are so very communicative through their eyes, tails and bodies in general. Be honest with yourself. Make a decision about your dog's care based on what is best for him. While we want our beloved dogs to be with us forever, there are times when their degree of suffering and diminished quality of life requires us to make tough decisions. Some experts believe the "harsh treatments" involved in fighting cancer in dogs are sometimes not the right path to take. In the words of Dr. Pitcairn:

> "...though chemotherapy, radiation, and surgery can have dramatic and rapid results, the quality of life for the animals afterward does not impress me. Life is more than just physical duration. To me it is not enough for the patient to be alive— there must also be some pleasure in that life. From the beginning of my career in veterinary medicine, I have been averse to the harsh treatments used for cancer. It just doesn't feel right to me. Further, I don't think that conventional treatment is effective in prolonging life. Recent evaluations of research into cancer treatment methods show that, contrary to popular belief, the overall death rate from cancer has stayed the same over the last 35 years....Considering the discomfort entailed in conventional treatment, I don't think it is worth it."

Once you understand what you are dealing with, what your options are and what you can commit to regarding the care of your dog, a decision typically will become clear. I personally feel that you know intrinsically what the right thing to do is, but you might second guess yourself or let your emotions take over. Whatever you do, *love, love, love* your dog. At the end of the day, it is all about your relationship with your best friend. Don't let him down. As hard as it may be for you, let him know how much you love him every minute of every day, through your touch, your words and your thoughts.

CHAPTER 4

Hospice Care

Let's take a look again at the definition of hospice care for animals from the Introduction: "Animal hospice is care for animals, focused on the patient's and the family's needs; on living life as fully as possible until the time of death [with or without intervention]; and on attaining a degree of preparation for death." According to the American Association of Human-Animal Bond Veterinarians, "hospice care for animals is a welcome additional option at the end of life. It is an alternative to premature euthanasia. It is also an alternative to prolonged suffering either in the isolation of intensive care or at home without treatment."

The goal of hospice care is to make the patient comfortable and provide as high a quality of life as possible, as well as give support to the patient's family. Hospice care comes into play when the patient is nearing the end of life. While most people are probably familiar with the availability of hospice care for humans, many are not aware that this approach is also very well suited to the care of our pet dogs.

For many owners, once cancer-related treatments have run their course and it is understood that the dog's condition is terminal, the decision is made at that point to euthanize the dog. Hospice care, by contrast, attempts to keep the dog comfortable until the dog dies a natural death or until a level of pain or discomfort becomes so great that euthanasia is warranted. To help you make the decision about which route is best for you and your dog, let's examine in more detail what hospice might involve.

Set your own priorities

One of the critical things I did was to develop a system to prioritize the elements of hospice care, much like Maslow's hierarchy of needs. (Maslow's hierarchy is a theory in psychology that categorizes the order of human needs by their necessity for survival. For example, a common interpretation of the hierarchy places physiological needs as most important, followed by security, love, esteem and potential.) This is a technique I used daily to approach the care of my dog in a way that reduced the stress of the situation for me and allowed me to focus on the most important aspects of his nutrition and daily ingestion of water, food, medicines and supplements.

Here is a visual representation of what I consider the hierarchy of needs for a dog with cancer during the hospice care period. You may have a different set of priorities.

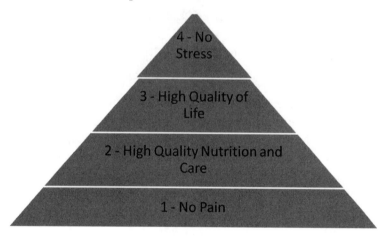

Based on my own experience, priorities and what I have come to learn, the basic elements of hospice care I recommend you use include the following:

- Providing pain management.

- Ensuring proper nutrition and care.

- Providing as high a quality of life as possible in terms of physical comfort, exercise and playtime.

- Minimizing stress.

Pain management

In order to manage pain, you need to be able to recognize when your dog is in pain. The International Veterinary Academy of Pain Management (IAVPM) provides a forum for communication of best practices of pain management for animals. According to the IAVPM, pain in dogs can be observed in four ways:

- Changes in posture, including anything abnormal or unusual for your dog in terms of position while sleeping, lying down, sitting or anything that looks as if the dog might be guarding a part of his body.

- Anything abnormal in your dog's movement, i.e., walking, getting up or lying down or anything unusual such as trembling or shaking.

- Changes in vocalization, such as moaning, whining, growling, barking or silence that is unusual for any given situation

- Changes in behavior: acting out of character; engaging in any unusual behavior; displaying agitation; excessive licking; or breaking house training (in trained dogs).

Once you recognize that your dog is in pain, you will want to act quickly. In the medical field, nurses and doctors often use a "PAIN" acronym to describe their methodology to approach pain management, which is applicable to hospice care. The following diagram captures this approach and can be adopted for animal hospice care as well.

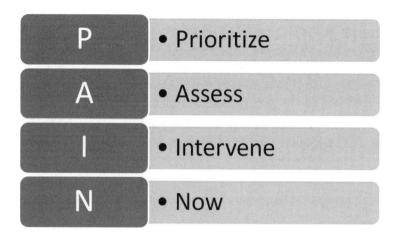

P • Prioritize

A • Assess

I • Intervene

N • Now

Pain medications and treatments

Of primary importance to me was that my dog experience as little pain as possible and to control related symptoms such as nausea and vomiting. Medications designed to treat pain are of critical importance for your dog, and you need to learn the right way to use them. Be sure to ask your veterinary team why they are prescribing one medication over another so that you can learn as much as you can about your dog's treatment plan. Some of the medicines discussed below were originally created to treat other diseases like depression or Parkinson's disease, and you should be aware of their potential side effects.

Ask your veterinarian for appropriate painkillers and instructions on how to administer them when your dog is in pain, especially during times when your veterinarian is unavailable. The last thing you want is for your dog to be in pain unnecessarily and not be able to do anything about it. Make sure to ask your veterinarian which drugs are still safe to use once your dog is no longer eating and also may no longer want to swallow. In addition, always verify which medicines can be given in concert and which cannot be combined. Many of the drugs that are prescribed for dogs can be purchased less expensively through retail outlets like Costco (always ask as these medicines are not necessarily listed or advertised on store websites).

With all of these drugs, be sure to work with your veterinarian on the proper dose for your dog, the maximum possible dose you could give if pain increases and how soon you could repeat such a dose. Some of the more common painkilling drugs will require a prescription from your veterinarian that you can then administer to your dog per the instructions you are provided:

- Non-Steroidal Anti-Inflammatory Drugs, or NSAIDs, such as carprofen (Rimadyl), deracoxib (Deramaxx), meloxicam (Metacam), etodolac (EtoGesic) and others

- Tramadol (Ultram), a synthetic opioid. It can be combined with NSAIDs.

- Acetaminophen (Tylenol) with codeine, a common pain reliever and fever reducer.

- Neurontin (Gabapentin) is an anticonvulsant medication, but is also used for chronic pain. It can be combined with NSAIDs.

- Some drugs like amitriptyline (Elavil) and amantadine can be used with other pain killers, including NSAIDs. They are not pain killers themselves, but instead increase the effect of a painkiller.

Other drugs and therapies can only be administered by vets, such as medicines in the opioid family. Dr. Mark Epstein of TotalBond Veterinary Hospitals in North Carolina wrote an article in December 2011 suggesting that "synthetic opioids remain powerful and perhaps one of the most useful tools for managing pain," although he says that many veterinarians avoid their use due to fear of their adverse side effects, such as extremely slow and/or shallow breathing and depression (exhibited through vocalization). According to Dr. Epstein, there are three classes of opioids: strong opioids such as morphine, oxymorphone, hydromorphone, methadone, fentanyl (Duragesic); weak opioids such as buprenorphine and butorphanol; and reversal agents such as naloxone, which is used to reverse cases of overdose. Morphine may be a drug option for dogs experiencing severe pain. Be aware that not every veterinarian is equipped to dispense opioids, and those who are may have strict guidelines under which they will supply these drugs for pain control in your dog. Pamidronate Drip

Therapy requires an all-day office visit and is useful for certain kinds of cancer, such as bone cancers. The treatment helps to strengthen bone by reducing calcium loss and also reduces pain.

Controlling nausea and vomiting

Nausea and vomiting often affect dogs suffering from pain. Medications and techniques to counter the effects of nausea include:

- **Cerenia.** This drug requires a prescription from your veterinarian.

- **Nux vomica** (a homeopathic remedy). One to five pellets placed in your dog's jowls, depending on size.

- **Ginger.** Your local natural food store will likely carry ginger in a pill form that can be used to combat nausea.

- **Acupressure.** Ask a holistic veterinarian about how to apply pressure to specific points to relieve symptoms such as nausea. (See Chapter 6 for more details on how to do this.)

For vomiting, the best advice is to restrict food intake, offer water and then contact your veterinarian at first opportunity. Pepto-Bismol might work for your dog, but ask your veterinarian for appropriate dosages.

Additional tips on pain medicine and management

Dr. Ella Bittel, in her *Spirits in Transition* weekend seminars and online classes, suggests that animal caretakers keep the following in mind when it comes to pain medicines and management:

- Never give your dog medicines that are intended for people unless directed by your veterinarian. They can be very dangerous for your dog.

- Never give your dog both steroids (such as prednisone, prednisolone, methylprednisolone, dexamethasone, triamcinolone) *and* NSAIDs (such as Rimadyl, Deramaxx, Metacam, EtoGesic, Previcox, Zubrin). Find out from your veterinarian how many days your dog has to be off the currently given drug before starting on the new one when intending to switch from steroids to NSAIDS or vice versa.

- Never give medicine at a higher dose, or more frequently, than prescribed. Particularly during end-of-life care, make sure you know from your veterinarian which medicines she prescribed for pain or seizures, vomiting or breathing difficulties and what the highest dose is that you can still safely administer if discomfort increases at a time when the veterinarian cannot be reached right away. Also clarify with your veterinarian how soon such a dose could be repeated if needed.

- When changing from one NSAID to another, it is also necessary to wait an appropriate number of days in between to allow the first drug to completely eliminate from the body, so as not to create complications. Again, clarify the appropriate time period through your veterinarian. You may need to use alternative pain medications during this time.

- If your dog has been taking steroids for some time and you want to stop because they no longer seem to be benefiting your dog, ensure you do not stop the medicine abruptly—a weaning off period is required. Sudden discontinuation of steroids after long-term use can be very harmful.

- As with humans, chronic pain in animals is often better controlled when pain medications are given on a regular schedule versus "give as needed." This provides your dog with consistent pain relief and thus often allows for lower doses to be more effective than otherwise. Once your dog's pain level reaches a peak, it is more difficult to remedy and likely to require higher doses and/or stronger medication. You want to prevent your dog from experiencing a peak of pain repeatedly. Instead, strive for your dog to be as consistently close to pain-free as possible.

- A combination of different medicines and modalities may yield better pain control with lower doses of each drug and with fewer side effects. The key is to work closely with your veterinarian to find the ideal combination for your dog.

- Especially if your dog is no longer eating much, or you know he has a sensitive tummy, consider alternatives to oral medicines with your vet such as injectable, transdermal, subcutaneous and sublingual medicines. Animals respond differently to various transmissions of medicines. For example, if your dog is suffering from nausea, it will be very difficult to entice him with oral medicines, even when disguised in his favorite treats. Find the method that works best for your situation.

- In some cases, controlled substances such as morphine or other opioids may be the best way to control your dog's pain. Note that not every veterinarian is licensed to dispense these drugs, and those who are must closely monitor and account for their use. Nonetheless, you need to be prepared to respond efficiently to a sudden increase in pain in your dog should it occur when veterinary care is not available in a timely manner, so work out a "Plan B" with your veterinarian before you may need it.

- Don't settle easily for "nothing else can be done." Something else usually can be done, but not every veterinarian is comfortable applying more complex pain management protocols or is trained to engage in hospice. If your regular veterinarian does not provide you with the help you need and is not open to consult with colleagues specializing in those areas, try to find another until you're satisfied that your dog is getting the needed support.

Alterative pain management techniques

Explore natural, complementary methods that you can employ at home to soothe pain. Here are some examples:

- The Castor Oil Wrap, originally developed by Edgar Cayce. This method, which uses castor oil in combination with moist heat, relieves bodily pains and detoxifies the liver. More details can be found here: http://www.cayce.com/castoroil.htm. The ingredients include: warmed castor oil (in a glass or stainless steel pan); very thin cotton fabric that is wide enough to fit around your dog's midsection; plastic wrap to fit around the fabric; a bucket of hot water; and cloth towel large enough to fit over the plastic wrap and fabric. A plastic tablecloth or old shower curtain can be used to protect the surface your dog is on from moisture. The method involves soaking the cloth with warm castor oil. Then, with your dog lying on his/her right side, wrap the cloth around the midsection and back. Cover with plastic wrap. Wet the towel with hot water, wring out and place over the plastic wrap. Leave this on for twenty minutes, reheating the towel if it starts to cool off. Repeat this every day, alternating sides for five days. On day six, separate from feeding time, give one tablespoon olive oil for a large dog or one teaspoon olive oil for a small dog.

- Mary Calanni of the Big Mountain Wildlife Animal Sanctuary in Guffey, Colorado created a pain remedy for her animals that consists of hyaluronic acid (for joint pain), white willow bark (the original aspirin), devil's claw (an herb), yucca (a plant), and MSM (methylsulfonylmethane, a supplement often used for joints). The combination of devil's claw and yucca is known to be a substitute for a very strong pain medication called phenylbutazone, which can cause ulcers. Consult your veterinarian regarding the possibility of using these supplements.

- The Tellington TTouch method, developed by Linda Tellington-Jones, http://www.lindatellingtonjones.com, can be used to relieve physical pain as well as to enhance comfort and a sense of well-being.

- Acupressure. Have a veterinarian trained in acupressure teach you points that are particularly helpful. A Canine Meridian chart can be purchased from Tallgrass Publishers, LLC (http://www.animalacupressure.com/Page.aspx?ID=239). They give courses as well.

- From the perspective of Energy Medicine, pain is caused by congested energy. One of the numerous techniques to relieve such congestion taught by Donna Eden for humans may also work for your dog: Place your left hand gently on your dog in the area of the pain, while pointing your right hand toward the ground. Visualize the pain moving from your dog through your body, and off of your right hand to the floor.

- Emotional pain can be as bothersome as physical pain. Flower essences, such as Bach flower essences can be helpful in moving through emotional challenges. Honeysuckle can help when we find ourselves thinking things could still be the way they were in the past; it can therefore also be useful when loved ones are dying or have died. These remedies are helpful not only for your dogs, including family dogs who may grieve the loss of their canine buddy, but for you as well. I frequently used both Honeysuckle and Rescue Remedy during my canine cancer experiences.

Create a hospice toolkit

An important element of hospice care is to be prepared. One way that you can do this is by creating a first aid toolkit that you can use when the need arises. The first step is to discuss the following questions with your veterinarian:

1. What kind of symptoms and side effects can I expect from this type of cancer?

2. How will the progression of the disease manifest itself?

3. What kind of symptoms and side effects can I expect during hospice care?

4. How will I recognize that my dog is nauseous?

5. How do I recognize that my dog is in pain?

6. How can I differentiate between my dog being nervous or anxious versus being in pain? Unfortunately, many dogs hide their pain and so it can be difficult to assess.

7. What can I give to my dog to alleviate symptoms/side effects, such as pain, nausea or anxiety?

Once you have discussed these questions with your veterinarian, you can create a first-aid toolkit to address the list of possible medical ailments that your dog might face, such as nausea, diarrhea, pain, anxiety, etc. It's particularly important that you gather these supplies as quickly as possible, as you don't want to find yourself in need of assistance on Saturday evening at 10 pm when your regular veterinarian is not available.

We've already discussed pain medication and treatments and how to address nausea and vomiting. You might also consider adding the following items to your toolkit:

- **Rescue Remedy**. This is a combination of Bach flower essences that is commonly sold at health food stores. Read more about this very popular remedy at the Bach site, http://www. bachflower.com/Rescue_Remedy.htm. In mild cases, this is a good, easy way to calm your dog—and you! Other handy Bach flower essences useful for pets can be found here: http:// bachflower.com/Pets.htm

- **Fast-Balance GI**. An easy to administer, good-tasting medicine to relieve diarrhea in your dog. It comes in a tube that allows you to control the amount that is dispensed. It can be purchased from your veterinarian or from online pet pharmacies. More info on their website: http://www.vetriscience. com/fastbalance.php

There might also be other medications to have on hand, depending on the type of cancer you are facing. For example, with mast cell tumor cancer, your veterinarian may suggest:

- **Pepcid AC**. Combats the enzymes that are released.
- **Sudafed**. Combats the histamines that are released.

> *When filling a prescription, try the Costco Pharmacy first, to see if they carry what your dog has been prescribed. You may be able to save a lot of money.*

As you care for your dog, you may be asked by your veterinarian to bring in stool or urine samples. Be sure to clarify the exact quantity that is needed so that you bring an amount that is sufficient for the testing. While getting a stool sample from your dog is easy, the idea of getting a urine sample might seem next to impossible. Here's my tip to getting a sample on the first try. You'll need: a disposable latex glove; a small plastic container with tight fitting lid (i.e., Gladware, etc.); and a plastic baggie with a tight closure (Ziploc bag). A shallower container will work better for female dogs. Put the glove on, have the container ready, and take your dog for a walk on his leash.

As s/he is urinating, place the cup under the stream and get a sample. Immediately put the lid on and place the entire container into the baggie, closing it. This worked for me every time.

High quality nutrition and care during hospice

The issues of nutrition and physical care for a dog with cancer are so important that I have devoted the next two chapters to this subject (Chapter 5, Diet and Nutrition; and Chapter 6, Massage, Sleep, Exercise and More). However, I have included the basics of what is needed in a hospice environment in the remainder of this chapter.

Here is what I recommend you provide your dog in terms of diet and nutrition during the period of hospice care:

1. **Pure or filtered water, fresh daily**. As long as your dog is still drinking fresh water every day, this is a good sign. It is preferable to provide filtered water rather than straight tap water for your dog.

   If you are concerned that your dog may be dehydrated, you can check to see if this is the case with the following technique: very gently pick up the skin on your dog's neck between or behind the shoulder blades and then let go. If the skin goes back down immediately, your dog is hydrated; if not, your dog is dehydrated. If your dog resists at all, stop right away.

2. **Food**. Your dog needs energy to fight the cancer, so it is critical that he have a diet sufficient for his weight. Ensuring that the food you give him is natural and unprocessed as well as high in protein is important. That said, any changes that you make to your dog's diet should be made gradually so as to not upset his digestive system and create unnecessary stress on his body. If your dog only eats a food such as dry kibble that is highly processed, try gradually switching to a more natural, grain-free alternative. Note: I fed my dogs a very high quality, grain-free, organic dry kibble recommended by my veterinarian. About two weeks into our two month battle

with cancer, my dog refused to eat it any more. I had to improvise after that point. Some options for protein are:

- Raw meats (organic).

- Cooked fish (always wild, never farmed).

- Cooked eggs (organic).

- Wet/canned dog food (organic, grain-free, natural ingredients).

- Dry dog kibble (organic, grain-free, natural ingredients).

- Seacure (pre-digested fish protein). Seacure is high in protein, yet very easily digestible.

And some options for vegetables and fruits are:

- Many vegetables have cancer fighting properties including broccoli, kale, sweet potatoes and beets.

- Avoid vegetables with high sugar content, like potatoes or corn.

- Avoid fruits with a lot of natural sugar, like bananas and apples.

- Try berries like strawberries, blueberries, raspberries, and blackberries.

Providing proper nutritional care for my dogs at home was time consuming in the beginning, especially when I was first adjusting their meals and daily care rituals to accommodate their cancer care. Early meals took me an hour to prepare, largely because I myself was largely unprepared for what to expect. I did not always have the right ingredients on hand, nor did I have a backup plan in place, when the first meal I provided was not eaten. Once I understood how appetite can be affected by cancer, I learned to have alternate meal options on hand and I also prepared meals in advance on the weekends so that I would not have to prepare everything from scratch during the week. By the time my second dog was diagnosed with cancer, I was well-prepared and his meals did not require more than a few minutes a day of additional preparation time.

If your dog has any other medical condition that requires that s/he takes medicine on a frequent basis, it is important to ensure that this medicine is continued. The last thing you want is to either compromise your dog's immune system or complicate his prognosis with another disease. For example, one of my dogs took thyroid medicine on a daily basis; it was important that he maintain this medicine. He also took Chinese herbs to control his epilepsy; I did my best to ensure that he continued to take these medicines as I did not want to complicate the situation by having the seizures return.

Depending on what type of disease your dog may have, you may consider working with your veterinarian to ensure that no unnecessary vaccinations are given to your dog. If your dog has or has had cancer, your veterinarian can write a letter that will exempt a dog from the only legally required vaccine, which is rabies. You certainly don't want to compromise your dog's immune system with a vaccination while he has cancer. According to Dr. Pitcairn, this is like "pouring gasoline on a fire." I also recommend you review Dr. Jean Dodds's Canine Vaccination Protocol to ensure that you are not vaccinating more than you need to (see the Resources section for more details).

As you'll read in Chapter 5, there are many different supplements that you can use to help your dog fight the battle against cancer. The specific supplements and herbs that you use should be discussed with your veterinarian and will depend on the type of cancer your dog is facing. Make sure you resist the urge to give your dog too many supplements at once. Also try to tailor the supplement to the type of cancer, how it manifests itself and how it is being treated. For example, if your dog is undergoing chemotherapy, milk thistle would be a good supplement as it will help support the liver in dealing with the toxins from the chemotherapy treatments.

It's a good idea to select a supplement that will boost your dog's immune system, as cancer only develops through a breakdown in the immune system. If chemotherapy is a part of your treatment plan, such supplements are very important, as chemotherapy is known to weaken the immune system.

Providing a high quality of life and reducing stress

These subjects are covered in detail in Chapter 6. In brief, the main elements are:

- Exercise
- Massage
- Grooming
- Maintaining a positive and cheerful outlook
- Stress reduction

Building a hospice care team

Similar to the human hospice model, it is common to work with a team of professionals for animal hospice. Working with a team should build confidence and give additional support to you, the main caregiver, and your family. This team might include:

- Your regular veterinarian.
- A veterinarian with a different specialty than your regular veterinarian, such as Western, holistic, homeopathic, acupuncture, etc.
- A veterinary specialist, including an oncologist, internist, etc.
- An animal body worker who can provide TTouch, Healing Touch, etc.
- An animal caregiver, who can provide special attention to your pet during the day when you are at work or who can take care of your pet when you are out of town.
- A grief therapist, who can assist you with the mourning process.

Preparing for death

Unfortunately hospice care and death are cruelly linked. You will want to know as much as possible about what I term "natural dying" and euthanasia to be able to make the decisions that only you can make. Being prepared to face what is coming before it actually happens will help give you the confidence to move forward. In Chapter 8 you will learn how to recognize the stages of natural death so that you can assess where your dog is on that journey. While euthanasia is not necessarily a goal of hospice care, there are times when hospice care ends with euthanasia.

The person who is closest to the dog is the ultimate decision maker, and is, with proper education, best suited to assess the dog's level of discomfort and suffering. It's my belief that you have to feel absolute certainty about a decision to euthanize. If there is any doubt, then it isn't time yet. Recall the first paragraph in Chapter 3, where we learned that our criteria for will-to-live are likely different from those of our canine companions. If your dog is happy to see you and be with you, then I'd argue that his will-to-live is still strong. You can ensure that he is as comfortable and pain-free as possible.

> There is a fine balance that occurs when administering hospice care. On the one hand, you want to ensure that your dog has all of the benefits of nutrition – food, water, medicines – to help in battling the disease. On the other hand, you do not want to interfere with the natural dying process. I knew nothing at all about dying with my first canine cancer experience, so it is possible that I prolonged the process by forcing food and water when it was not really necessary. In a natural death, as the body starts to shut down, food and water are no longer required, and yet, this does not cause discomfort within your pet. With my second canine cancer experience, I was able to recognize each stage of the natural dying process as we experienced it, and could assess whether food, water, or medicine was needed. More detail on the natural dying process can be found in Chapter 8.

Even if you are committed to helping your dog along a path to a natural death, be prepared for the possibility that the end might not come naturally. Recall that two of my recommended goals for hospice care are minimization of pain and maximization of quality of life. However, if you are faced with a situation where your dog is suffering extreme pain or his quality of life is not a level that you feel comfortable with, then opting for euthanasia could be the best option. Sometimes life throws us a curve ball, and things do not always work out the way we'd like. As a parallel example, when my son was born, I very much wanted an unmedicated ("natural") birth, with no pain medicines or other interventions. What actually happened was that I wound up having almost every intervention in the book, so to speak, and ultimately he was born via a Caesarean section. This was absolutely not what I intended, but in the end, was the best option given the specific circumstances that I was dealt. Life and death do not always play out in the way we desire. Having flexibility and always keeping your dog's needs at the highest priority are extremely important when administering hospice care.

There may come a point in your hospice care that you feel as though your dog might be lingering, instead of progressing toward a natural death. If your dog is heavily dependent on medications, such as steroids, for example, it is possible that they may be delaying the ultimate outcome. In some cases, this may be desired, but in other cases, where the quality of life is not high, this might be counterproductive. You may consider, in such a situation, working with your veterinarian to create a plan to slowly wean your dog off of these medicines, so that he may progress towards a natural death, in his own time.

> If you suspect that your dog is lingering, you can administer the homeopathic remedy Arsenicum album 30C, which is sold at natural health food markets, to assist your dog in moving on. There is some debate between classical homeopathic and other veterinarians as to the effects of this remedy if your dog is not ready to go naturally. Consult with your veterinarian for more information.

A few words on euthanasia

If your dog's quality of life becomes very poor during active dying, and he does not appear to be ready to progress towards a natural death, the option of euthanasia is available. Make sure that the licensed veterinarian you work with uses a two-step procedure for euthanasia, as follows:

- Step 1. Administer a sedative, either by injection or tablet. This ensures that your dog will be comfortable and pain free during the procedure. The elimination of this step can cause complications. Not all vets take this step, so please inquire before agreeing to the procedure.

- Step 2. Administer a euthanasia drug, which is essentially an overdose of a barbiturate. It is injected directly into a vein or via an IV catheter.

Each euthanasia experience will not be identical. If you have questions or concerns about the process, discuss them with your veterinarian. You can also inquire as to whether your veterinarian will consider an in-home euthanasia experience. If not, you may want to find a veterinarian who does provide in-home service, so that option is available to you should your path lead to that outcome.

The outlook for hospice care for animals

Hopefully, as the interest in animal hospice continues, we will see an increase in the availability of animal hospice services, and perhaps, someday, courses on animal hospice care will be taught in veterinary schools. One potential obstacle, however, may come from veterinarians themselves. Dr. Guy Hancock, DVM, MEd, writes this about animal hospice care: "The veterinarian must first recognize that the patient is terminal and that hospice care is a better alternative than further heroic attempts at cure. This step is complicated by the veterinarian's emotional investment in the case's good outcome, which may make it more difficult to admit the true circumstances as early as is optimal. In addition to determining the appropriate time to make a switch to hospice care, a second problem is that there is no veterinary hospice to which a referral can be made. The same veterinarian must re-evaluate the patient care plan from an entirely different perspective. The veterinarian, veterinary technician, and clients should jointly develop a plan of care to address relief of pain and management of signs. Clients should be made aware of various techniques that might be employed, and their limitations. They should be advised of signs indicating pain, side effects of the medical conditions and treatments, and anticipated complications as the patient's condition declines. Clients may need to decide if euthanasia is still an option, how the pet's remains will be treated after death, and other details of care and memorialization."

To further the cause of animal hospice, Dr. Ella Bittel Bittel and many other veterinarians have helped to form a non-profit organization called the International Association of Animal Hospice and Palliative Care. Its mission is to:

- Increase awareness of the availability of animal hospice and palliative care for pet owners.

- Create guidelines for animal hospice and palliative care that can be used by veterinarians and other animal service providers.

- Provide an opportunity for those involved in animal hospice and palliative care to share their research and experience for the benefit of all.

- Ensure that animal hospice and palliative care is recognized as an area of specialty for those practicing in the field.

I chose to employ hospice-type care with both of my canine cancer experiences even though I did not know much about the concept of hospice initially. In both cases, the cancers were quite advanced by the time I figured out what was happening. Surgeries were not an option, partially due to the locations of the tumors, but more due to the fact that the cancers had metastasized. I could have opted in both cases for chemotherapy, but in neither case would this have resulted in an eradication of the cancer or a significant increase in lifespan. The approach that felt right to me was to enjoy the time that I had left with my dog and to focus on ensuring that he had a good quality of life throughout. It wasn't until I'd started writing this book and researching canine cancer and treatment options that I realized that what I had done with my dog was indeed hospice care. And, in retrospect, I believe that it was the best choice for both me and my dogs.

CHAPTER 5
Diet and Nutrition

When your beloved pet is faced with cancer, some of your most valuable allies will be the foods and nutrients that you can give to help strengthen him, as well as to deter the growth of the cancer. In the previous chapter, I mentioned briefly some aspects of dietary need during hospice care. In this chapter, I will go into more detail regarding diet and nutrition recommendations that are relevant no matter what stage of the fight against cancer you are in; you can use these as they are or adapt to suit your pet's tastes and the foods that are available to you. The strategies that you adopt will depend on the type of cancer your dog has and what treatment options you have chosen to follow. For example, if your dog is undergoing chemotherapy, this will take a toll on his immune system, bone marrow and intestinal tract. Feeding your dog foods and supplements that can counteract these effects will be critical in helping your dog.

Diet can play a strong role in the outcome of cancer treatment in dogs. Take care to evaluate your dog's current diet, and work with a veterinarian to develop a diet that will be suitable for your dog. If you remember anything about cancer and diet, it should be this: *Cancer cells thrive on sugar, but they do not metabolize fats.* So your overall strategy should be to feed your dog a diet high in fats and protein and low in carbohydrates. Doing so will starve the cancer, yet continue to nourish your dog.

Overall, you want to present your dog with a diet that has these following characteristics:

- High protein.
- High fiber.
- High fatty acids.
- Low carbohydrates.
- Natural, organic and unprocessed foods.

There are many resources on the web that can provide you with very detailed information regarding how to prepare meals for your dog from scratch, whether raw or cooked. Reputable resources can be found in the Appendix.

Foods to feed and foods to avoid

Consult with your veterinarian if you choose to feed a commercial natural pet food brand. She may recommend you supplement your dog's diet with vegetables, fruit and soy products to include foods that are natural cancer inhibitors. Here are some known cancer-fighting food options:

- Cruciferous vegetables, like cabbage, Brussels sprouts, broccoli and cauliflower. These foods contain phytonutrients, which work with antioxidants to protect cells from free radical damage, increase the production of enzymes that prevent the formation of malignant tissue and stop carcinogens from DNA mutation. They also contain sulforaphane which is known to have anti-cancer properties.

- Soy products, like tempeh, tofu, miso and soy milk. These foods contain enistein, an antioxidant that helps prevent damage from free radicals, and isoflavones, which stop the creation of the blood vessels that supply cancer cells.

- Vegetables in the onion family, like garlic, scallions, shallots, leeks and chives. These foods contain allicin which stimulates the immune system and slows tumor growth.

- Flaxseed, flaxseed oil and fish oil. These foods contain lignans, plant compounds that behave like estrogen and may protect the body from cancer, and essential fatty acids, such as alpha-linoleic acid and Omega-3 fatty acids, which have been found to reduce the risk of certain types of cancers. Found in fish oil, Omega-3 fatty acids can "inhibit the matrix metalloproteinase (MMP) enzymes that play a role in how cancer cells survive and spread in the body" according to Dr. Messonnier.

- Vegetables and fruits that contain carotenoids like the beta-carotene in sweet potatoes, carrots, apricots, cantaloupe, squash, peaches, spinach, kale and the lycopene in tomatoes, which are antioxidants believed to be helpful in the prevention of cancer, are good dietary choices. Beta-carotene is known to be a cancer preventive when consumed as part of a normal diet. Lycopene prevents uncontrolled growth of cancer cells. These foods can help prevent cancer of the larynx, esophagus and lungs.

- Grapes. Grapes contain Resveratrol which help to block the formation and growth of tumors.

- Because cat food is higher in fat and protein than most dog foods, Dr. Shawn Messonnier recommends finding a holistic brand of canned cat food if your dog resists other high protein and high fat options.

- Fiber, such as bran, psyllium and pumpkin. Fiber helps slow down the absorption of sugar from the diet. Psyllium works really well as a thickening agent (see the Doggie Quiche recipe later in this chapter).

There are also foods that you should avoid:

- Simple sugars and carbohydrates, found in foods like pasta, white rice, bread and cereals. Feeding these foods to your dog is not recommended since they have little or no nutritional value.

- Non-organic animal fat from chicken, beef, etc. These non-nutritional fats contain Omega-6 fatty acids, which are known to promote the growth of cancer and have even been shown to enhance metastasis. Note that grass-fed beef contains Omega-3 fatty acids, so if you feed beef, try to make it grass-fed.

- Most traditional commercial dog food. There are too many additives, salt and potentially contaminated sources in commercial pet food today. It's too risky to feed this to a healthy pet, never mind a pet that is battling cancer.

- Processed foods. If you didn't plant it, harvest it or raise it yourself, question it. Do you really know where it came from and what was used to produce it? Is it worth the risk to feed your dog something that might potentially harm him, and at the very least, anything that is not going to provide some nutritional benefit? Don't waste calories during this crucial time. In particular, avoid foods preserved with ethoxyquim, butylatedhydroxytoluene (BHT) and/or sodium nitrate.

Watch out for changes in appetite and eating habits

It was only a couple of weeks after the cancer diagnosis that my dog refused to eat dry kibble. I switched to frozen meats and canned meats (recommended by my veterinarian), but these only interested him for another week or two. After that point, I was pretty much on my own, and so within the guidelines provided to me by our veterinarian, I adapted human foods to meet his dietary requirements. It is no secret that dogs with cancer have heightened senses, which results in their more likely refusal of foods and medicines that they might have been inclined to eat ordinarily. In addition, depending on the treatment that your dog is undergoing, he might just not feel well from the treatment and lose his appetite as a result.

> *Important: It is critical to keep a daily log of what your dog has eaten each day, including medicines and supplements, as well his activities, behaviors and treatments. This is essential in being able to identify any unusual behaviors that might be related to foods, supplements, medicines or treatments. For example, if your dog has an acupuncture treatment one day, and is romping about happily the next, this might indicate that he responds well to the treatment. This information will be invaluable during your visits to your veterinarian.*

In my case, I very quickly realized that what I wanted my dog to eat, what he wanted to eat, and what he actually would eat, were three very different things. This was my first time deviating from the back of the package to tell me how much of what to give him. From a volume perspective, I tried to mimic the amount of food I had used before. If I used to give him three cups of dry kibble, then he got at least three cups of homemade food, including meat and veggies, as found in the recipes below. I belong to a local CSA (Community Supported Agriculture) and every week I would get a fresh, organic selection of fruits and vegetables that I would then parlay into portions of his weekly meals.

You will very likely have to deal with a dog who becomes increasingly finicky in his tastes and the amount of food he wants to eat. The progression of cancer, as with most terminal diseases, is often accompanied by a progressive loss of appetite and general disinterest in food, even foods that once were absolutely irresistible. This is where your creativity and ingenuity come in. With my experiences, I invented recipes and tried to cook the most nutritious, appetizing meals I could muster. I tried to be as creative as possible in enticing my dogs to, at minimum, take medicines. I used peanut butter, cream cheese, steak, chicken, bacon, sausage…anything that would even remotely spark his interest. There were days that I could not get my dog to take any medicine, including necessary medicines, regardless of how tantalizing the delivery mechanism was.

Unfortunately, it took me a while to develop this approach and refine it into a daily routine. For example, initially, our mealtimes would take 60 to 90 minutes from start to finish, as I'd try to prepare his meals the way I'd always done so in the past. Many mealtimes ended in tears when I'd realize that, in spite of my efforts, he'd not eaten anything that he needed to eat. I gradually realized that I needed to be more prepared at each mealtime, with several options that I could easily switch amongst in case he was finicky that day. Once I had shifted my mindset about mealtimes and realized that flexibility was key, I was able to narrow down a more palatable meal choice within 15 to 20 minutes. Remember to be easy on yourself as you are adjusting to hospice care; the more you use this approach, the better you will get at reading your dog and making adjustments to his daily care.

> *What I wish I knew at the beginning of this process was that dogs with cancer don't necessarily want to eat the same things every day. What tastes great to them one day will not be appetizing the next day. This is also typical of animals that are close to the end of their lives. Porter's lack of interest in eating food that I gave him was not a reflection on me and what/how I was trying to feed him; it was a result of the fact that his taste buds were changing daily as his body attempted to ward off the cancer. I eventually learned that I needed to have a variety of meal options on hand every single day. Once I accepted this fact, mealtimes became a lot easier. This also meant that I needed to do my preparation for mealtimes in a much more efficient and timely manner. I made bulk amounts of various vegetables and meats, so that I would have several options in terms of combining both to make a healthy meal.*

As your dog gets more finicky, the meals you can get him to eat by necessity may not be a perfect balance of meat and veggies. Some days, my dog wanted all meat and nothing else. Other days, he went for everything I gave him. The key is to always be flexible and let him choose what he wants. When it comes to food, most dogs are pretty smart with their sense of smell, so you are likely not going to get anything past them that is not appealing on any given day. That makes it hard to disguise anything in most foods, notably pills and medication. However, I was able to conjure up a few recipes that enabled me to give him his medicines in pill form, without him even knowing it. Unfortunately, I was not able to disguise the truly awful taste of Chinese herbs for very long. If I put even a half teaspoon in his food, he'd smell it and refuse to eat it. Authors Deb Eldredge and Margaret Bonham recommend that "sometimes warming the food in the microwave for a few seconds will make the food appetizing enough to eat." I did notice that Porter was more receptive to food generally when it was room temperature, not cold, straight from the refrigerator. With respect to microwaving, however, I'd exercise some caution there, as there is some evidence that microwaving modifies the molecular structure of food. To be perfectly safe, I recommend either leaving the food out at room temperature for 30 minutes or putting it in the oven for five to ten minutes.

If you do not normally feed your dog any raw food, this is not a good time to introduce it. If you do feed your dog raw food, you should consider cooking it first to provide an easier digestive experience. You may ask your raw food provider if they can create custom blends that contain higher percentages of proteins than carbohydrates, and perhaps supplements that will support your dog in staving off the cancer. Shelley Fuller of Paw's Café in Redmond, Washington creates custom cancer blends that can even be tailored to whether a dog is undergoing chemotherapy or not.

Using food to make the medicine go down

Generally the key to using food to encourage the dog to take his medicine involves finding something soft that you can use to wrap around the pill to encourage your dog to eat. Once you find something, cut it into bite-size squares. Then push one pill into each square and feed by hand to your dog. You may find it easier to have him sit or lie down and use the food square the pill inside as a "reward." My dogs have always loved to be rewarded for their good behavior, so treats after tricks are never regarded suspiciously.

Food square suggestions include:

- Doggie quiche (see recipe section later in this chapter).

- Cooked hamburger or meatloaf (see recipe section later in this chapter). Add minced carrot, broccoli, garlic and egg to meatloaf for added nutrition.

- Canned fish, such as herring filets and salmon.

- Sandwich meat/cheese (ensure that any meat you give to your dog is organic and contains no added preservatives such as nitrates).

- If you like to cook, try the "Sora's Goo" recipe found below, which uses all natural and tasty ingredients (thanks to Michelle Nichols, President of The Animal Hospice, End-of-Life, and Palliative Care Project in Bellevue, Washington for the recipe).

> *What I wish I had known at the beginning: my son ate ham and cheese sandwiches for school every day. I mistakenly thought that hiding some of my dog's pills in my son's expensive sandwich meat was a great way to get my dog to take his medicines. But then he started to have shaking spells where his head would shake uncontrollably for about a minute, and then stop. He'd already had epilepsy and so I thought that maybe the cancer had weakened his immune system to the point where the epilepsy was coming back. I happened to read an article in the interim about how nitrates can cause epileptic-type responses in children who are exposed to nitrates. I researched the sandwich meat that I fed to my son and realized that even though it was the most expensive brand you could find in the local grocery store, it contained nitrates. As soon as I eliminated that from my dog's diet, the uncontrollable head shaking never happened again. And I never fed my son that brand of ham. I later was able to find nitrate-free, organic lunchmeat at my local natural foods market.*

If the medicine you need to give your dog is in powdered form you can sprinkle it on the food from the recipes below or sprinkle it on either dry or wet kibble, whichever one your dog will eat at a given stage. It is important to note that my success rate with this method was extremely low. Having had Chinese herbs administered to me, I was well aware of the awful taste and so understood why my dog would not take them. There was no way that I found to disguise them sufficiently to fool him. I think each dog is different, and so you need to try as many options as you can find to see if yours will tolerate the taste.

Recipes containing recommended ingredients

The following recipes are for items that I found were helpful to have on hand, as they provided a healthy and nutritional variety of food at each mealtime, as well as provided a mechanism by which I could get medicine into my dog in the most unobtrusive way I could manage.

Doggie Quiche

- 4 eggs
- ½ cup rice milk
- 3 to 4 cups grated organic broccoli/cauliflower/carrots, or any combination of these
- 1 cup cooked organic ground beef or sausage
- 2 tbsp psyllium husk powder
- 1 cup parmigiano/reggiano grated cheese
- Sprinkle of pepper
- Sprinkle of nutmeg

In bowl, mix all ingredients through psyllium, and pour into pie dish. Sprinkle cheese, pepper and nutmeg on top and cook in a pre-heated oven at 350 degrees for 30 minutes.

Doggie Meatloaf

- 4 cloves organic garlic
- 1 organic carrot
- 1 cup organic broccoli
- ½ cup organic parsley
- ½ cup organic corn meal
- ½ cup ketchup
- 1 tsp freshly ground pepper
- 1 tsp fresh rosemary
- 2 lbs organic ground beef
- 2 organic eggs
- 2 to 3 strips or organic, nitrate-free bacon

In food processor, chop first four ingredients until finely chopped and place in a large bowl. Add next six ingredients to the bowl and using your hands, mix the ingredients well, but be careful to not over-mix. Place a wire baking rack into a pan and cover with parchment paper.

Arrange the mixture into a loaf shape on the parchment, covering with 2 to 3 strips of bacon over the top. Cook for an hour at 400 degrees in a preheated oven. A meat thermometer should read 160 degrees.

Scrambled Eggs

- 2 organic eggs
- 1 tsp psyllium husk powder
- 1 tsp mushroom powder
- ½ tsp each Chinese herb (if tolerated)
- ½ tbs organic olive oil

Heat oil in pan and add eggs. Scramble eggs with herbs/supplements and cook until eggs are fluffy and no longer runny and wet.

Creamy Salmon

- 2 cans cooked wild salmon (16 oz cans)
- 1 cup cream cheese, organic

Mix salmon and softened cream cheese until blended.

Mashed Butternut/Acorn Squash

- 1 lb organic butternut or acorn squash, peeled, seeded, and diced (frozen squash can be used instead)
- 2 qts water
- Organic chicken broth
- 1 tsp Herbes de Provence

Boil squash until soft, strain, add chicken broth, Herbes de Provence and mash until consistency of mashed potatoes is achieved.

Sautéed Kale or Chard

- 4 cups organic kale, chard, or similar greens
- 1 tbsp organic olive oil
- 1 tbsp garlic

Sauté garlic in oil and then add greens until wilted, but not soggy.

Baked Beets

- 1 lb organic beets (golden, orange or red)
- 1 tbsp organic olive oil
- Dash fresh grated black pepper

Peel and quarter beets and place into ovenproof baking dish. Drizzle olive oil over top, sprinkle pepper and bake for one hour at 375 degrees.

Sora's "Goo"

- ½ part honey
- 1 part peanut butter
- 1 part Nutiva coconut oil
- 1 part Nutiva hemp seed protein with fiber

Mix together and store in an airtight container. The mixture does not have to be refrigerated.

Using herbs and supplements

I am certain many of you have heard about the health benefits of Omega-3 fatty acids and antioxidants for humans in the battle against cancer. As it turns out, these supplements are also beneficial to dogs in their battle with cancer. Be certain to consult your veterinarian before using any of these supplements, however. According to Dr. Messonnier in his book *The Natural Vet's Guide to Preventing and Treating Cancer in Dogs*, "since antioxidants detoxify free radicals, which may cause or contribute to certain side effects that are common to many anti-cancer drugs, antioxidants may reduce or prevent many cancer therapy side effects. Most holistic veterinarians, and a growing number of conventional oncologists, support the proper use of antioxidants and other supplements before, during and after conventional treatment of the pet with cancer." The same guidance applies to the use of herbs in the battle against cancer. Messonnier writes that, "while herbs are generally safe, their active ingredients can have powerful effects. Don't use herbal therapy on your pet without proper veterinary supervision. "

Cancer-fighting herbs

In his book *The Natural Health Bible for Dogs and Cats*, Dr. Messonnier includes a very detailed description of the best cancer-fighting herbs, which I have summarized and grouped according to their healing properties. These include:

What it Supports	Herb	Description
Weight Gain	Alfalfa	An antioxidant that helps the dog to gain weight.
Bone Marrow	Aloe Vera	An antioxidant that stimulates the bone marrow.
Immune System	Astragalus	An antibacterial and anti-inflammatory herb used to strengthen the immune system.
	Cat's Claw	Works as an anti-inflammatory and stimulates the immune system.
	Echinacea	An antiviral and antibacterial herb with immune supporting properties.
	Ginseng	Acts as an antioxidant, stimulates the immune system and enhances white blood cell and antibody functions. This herb should be administered only under supervision of a veterinarian.

What it Supports	Herb	Description
Immune System, cont.	Licorice Root	A fast-acting anti-inflammatory agent, it is an anti-microbial and stimulates the immune system.
	Marshmallow	Combats irritation of the skin or mucous membranes, is antibacterial and stimulates the immune system.
	Mistletoe (also Anti-Cancer)	An herb which protects DNA, stimulates the immune system and encourages cell death, and acts as an anti-tumor and an anti-metastatic agent.
	Turmeric (also Anti-Cancer)	An herb which inhibits cancer growth, induces cancer cell death thereby inhibiting the spread of cancer. Also acts as an anti-inflammatory, antioxidant and stimulates the immune system.
	Wormwood (also Anti-Cancer)	An herb which controls infection, strengthens immunity and is particularly good at killing cancer cells because of their higher concentration of iron.
Blood	Burdock Root	A diuretic and blood cleanser.
	Red Clover	A tonic, diuretic and blood cleanser.

What it Supports	Herb	Description
Anti-Cancer	Flax	Contains fatty acids, lignans and anti-oxidants along with chemicals that have anti-pro-liferative, anti-estrogen and anti-angiogenesis properties.
	Garlic	An antioxidant, which stimu-lates white blood cell produc-tion and inhibits chemicals that help cancers grow.
Bladder/Gastro	Goldenseal	A topical antimicrobial and anti-inflammatory herb, help-ful for side effects caused by cancer therapies of the blad-der or gastrointestinal system.
Liver/Chemo	Dandelion	Works as an anti-inflammato-ry, stimulates the liver and is a diuretic.
	Hawthorn	An antioxidant, can combat cardiac side effects of some chemotherapy drugs.
	Milk Thistle	Protects the liver and reduces the toxicity of chemotherapy.
	Oregon Grape (also good for Blood)	An antimicrobial agent that supports liver function and stimulates white blood cell production.
	Yellow Dock	An herb that stimulates the liver, remedies anemia and cleanses bowels.
Cancer Treatment	Hoxsey and Essiac For-mulas	Antioxidants believed to be effective in treating cancer.

Cancer fighting supplements

Here is a list and description of cancer fighting supplements based on research I have completed from a large number of sources, most notably Dr. Messonnier's book, *The Natural Vet's Guide to Preventing and Treating Cancer in Dogs*. These include:

- **Omega 3 fatty acids**. A high-fat diet contains Omega-3 fatty acids. Flax seed oil, cod liver oil and fish oil are at the top of the list in terms of containing Omega-3 fatty acids. Flax seed oil has the highest Omega-3 fatty acid content but its Omega-6 fatty acids content, which is less helpful, is fairly high. When Omega-3 fatty acids are used nutritionally or in supplement form, antioxidants such as vitamin E should be given as well. This is also true for humans; my own doctor advised me to take vitamin E along with my fish oil pills. According to Dr. Messonnier, "fish oil contains the active Omega-3s DHE and EPA...I prefer to prescribe Omega-3s via fish oil."

- **Essiac tea**. This is a human grade formula that was originally developed by a Canadian nurse named Rene Caisse in the mid-1920s as a cure for cancer. It is said to originate from a local Native American tribe. The original recipe includes greater burdock root, slippery elm inner bark, sheep sorrel and Indian rhubarb root. For best results, use the original formula, as generic options have not undergone the same level of testing as the original. I have included the website listing in the Appendix on the history of Essiac Tea.

- **Colostrum**. This is found naturally in mother's milk of many species (and can be purchased in powdered or pill form). It supports and strengthens the immune system and it is critical for new born puppies.

- **Antioxidant formulas**. Some examples include Quercenol, which contains several flavonoids, milk thistle extract (supports the liver), and green tea polyphenols, which are antioxidants. Curcumin, found in the spice turmeric, is a powerful antioxidant. Resveratrol, a component of grape skins has received the seal of approval from the National Canine Cancer Foundation.

- **Lignans**. These are found in extra virgin olive oil and flaxseeds. Lignans act as antioxidants and have anti-cancer properties. According to Messonnier, "lignans contain seoisoloriciresinol diglycoside and matairesinol, which are active cancer-fighting chemicals that have anti-proliferative, anti-estrogen, and anti-angiogenesis properties, all of which may slow the growth and spread of cancer."

- **Chinese herbs**. Three herbs in particular are notable: (1) Wei Qi Booster, which supports the immune system; (2) Statis Breaker, which helps to shrink tumors; and (3) Yunnan Bai-yai Capsule which supports healthy blood flow and promotes clotting to stop excessive bleeding.

- **Maitake Mushrooms**. This is a Japanese mushroom used in traditional Chinese medicine which supports the immune system, is believed to have anti-metastatic properties and has been shown to inhibit the growth of some cancer cells as well as encourage apoptosis (cancer cell death).

- **M2 Mushroom Matrix** (see website listing in the Appendix). This product contains powerful anti-oxidative and enzyme properties, promotes oxidative stress support and supports natural immune agents.

- **Mushrooms**. A variety of mushrooms are commonly used to treat various medical ailments. They are known to have anti-bacterial, antiviral, immune-stimulating and anti-tumor characteristics that vary according to the type of mushroom used. Be sure to only administer mushrooms to your pets that are provided by your veterinarian as some mushrooms can be extremely toxic, both to dogs and people.

- **Glutamine**. This is an amino acid that assists in increasing muscle mass while decreasing the severity of gastrointestinal effects of chemotherapy.

- **Glycoproteins/glycoconjugate**. These sugars are proteins that can be used to treat liver tumors and have been known to decrease liver metastasis.

- **Lycopene**. This supplement is an antioxidant that is twice as effective as the more common beta-carotene (found in carrots, pumpkins, sweet potatoes and leafy greens, etc.). It is thought to reduce cancer in both pets and people, but detailed research has not been performed to determine optimal and safe dosages. Use with caution.

- **The Marsden Protocol**. This was developed by Dr. Steve Marsden, a veterinarian specializing in holistic medicine. When a dog owner refuses conventional therapy for his or her pet, this treatment can be used as an alternative, specifically for osteosarcoma, fibrosarcoma, lymphosarcoma, and squamous cell carcinoma. The protocol includes the following ingredients: Oregon grape root; burdock root; red clover flower; boneset herb; prickly ash bark; stillingia root; alfalfa leaf; cascara sagrada bark; poke root; and licorice root. While this protocol is considered promising, the number of dogs treated is not statistically significant to warrant its recommendation over more proven methods of treatment.

- **MDN-3**. This product contains extracts of several mushrooms in a shell composed of rice bran. It has immune-stimulating effects.

- **Noni**. This supplement comes from a plant found in the South Pacific and is available as a juice. It has antioxidant and immune-stimulating properties and may reduce some DNA damage.

There is an excellent white paper on page 155 that covers how nutrition can be used in prevention and recovery from canine cancer. The article was written by Shelly Fuller, owner and pet nutritionist at Paws Café in Redmond, Washington.

CHAPTER 6

Providing Your Dog a High Quality of Life While Fighting Cancer

Whether your dog is expected to recover from cancer treatment or you are providing hospice care, there are a number of things beyond the medical and nutritional treatments discussed in the previous chapters that you can do help provide him as high a quality of life as possible. Some are quite simple such as spending time with your dog, petting and talking with him. This does not need to require hours and hours of your time; even short periods of ten to fifteen minutes can have enormous benefits. Ideally, find time every day to massage or pet your dog in a stress-free environment, to provide your dog with the right amount of exercise for his current energy level and to perform any grooming activities that might be necessary, such as brushing, nail trimming or ear cleaning. Of course, if any of these activities are highly stressful for your animal, then do not force them. Work with your veterinarian to brainstorm ways to ensure that your dog's grooming needs can be fulfilled in a way that minimizes stress. These are the quality of life factors I recommend focusing on:

Exercise

Exercise can affect your dog's ability to combat cancer and heal. The ultimate goal is to create a balanced life. You want to make sure that your dog gets as much exercise as possible, but not to the detriment of his health and his ability to be strong enough to fight the cancer. For example, if you have an active schedule for your dog that does not allow him time to relax and get sufficient rest, you run the risk of creating a situation of fatigue and your dog's immune system may be compromised. Too little exercise may impact circulation and digestion. Again, this is an area where you are the expert on your dog and know better than anyone else what constitutes too much or too little physical exertion. Take into account other treatments that your dog may have recently had that might impact his ability to be active, like recent surgeries or chemotherapy treatments.

With my canine cancer experiences, there were days that we were able to enjoy 30 minute walks together and even trips to local dog parks where my dog swam and romped as if he were still a puppy.

But then there were days where making it to the end of the block seemed like a marathon task, and still others where we could only go as far as the end of the driveway and then we'd have to go back inside. Take into account your local weather as well. Temperature extremes may be more difficult for your dog, so take care not to go farther than he seems able or interested in going. If you think it is likely to rain or snow, you might want to plan a shorter route.

That said, I recommend the following guidelines for exercise:

- If you live in a cold climate, be mindful of the temperature when you are taking your dog for walks.

- Similarly, if you live in a wet climate or take your dog swimming, be sure to have plenty of dry towels on hand to dry him off, and warm blankets to wrap him up in afterwards.

- Carry a cell phone so that you are not stuck in a situation where your dog either won't, or is unable, to move. This way you can call family or friends for assistance.

- Be flexible; let your dog lead the way and determine how far he'd like to go. Don't force him farther than he can go comfortably.

- If you think that your remaining time with your dog is short, consider a visit to one of his favorite places where you can take some photos and create lasting memories of the two of you enjoying life together. Michelle Nichols, President and Founder of the Animal Hospice, End-of-Life, and Palliative Care Project (http://www.ahelpproject.org), took her dog Sora to a local dog park on a lovely fall day in the final months of Sora's life. The photos that were taken that day are treasured by Michelle and her family and allowed them to focus on the memories of Sora in her more healthful and youthful days.

Reducing stress
Have you created an environment within your home that is upbeat and cheerful, eliminating unnecessary stress for your dog? While some dogs handle stress better than others, this is not the time to be introducing any kind of changes into your dog's life; change, even

if small, can cause unintended stress. You can help your dog feel comfortable by sticking to familiar routines. Don't plan unnecessary outings or trips that might take you away from your dog. If you need to modify your dog's eating habits, avoid making the changes too quickly. Work with your veterinarian to ensure that you can institute dietary changes in a way that will not result in any digestive strains. According to Dr. Philip J. Bergman "if you decide to make some changes, do so slowly, one thing at a time, so that your pet has a chance to adjust. The stress that develops from having to adjust to too many changes at once can actually make a dog sicker. It can then become difficult to differentiate between the effects of a progression of the cancer versus changes in the home." This is wise advice; change is stressful for people as well as pets, so it will benefit the owner as well to stick to routine, at least initially, until an appropriate treatment plan is developed.

At the end of the day, any kind of stress is bad. This applies not only to emotional stress, but also to physical stress. You want your dog to be as strong as possible physically to be able to fight the cancer, but to still build his own resistance and endurance to weather the battle ahead. It can be difficult to manage, especially when you are already under a lot of stress yourself in dealing with cancer.

> It pays to invest in a small, hand-held carpet cleaning machine if you have carpet in your home. Dogs with cancer (and in general) will occasionally throw up, and it is best if you have tools on-hand to use to help with clean-up. This is part of helping to minimize your stress as well. Any stress you feel will invariably be picked up by your dog, and it is best if you can reduce or better, eliminate, this kind of vicarious stress.

Quality of sleep

Sleep is a critical component to healing. It is when we sleep that our bodies have a chance to relax and allow healing to take place. This is true in dogs, as it is with humans. Ensure that you create a peaceful and comfortable spot for your dog to sleep in. If your dog is older and also suffers from arthritis or hip dysplasia, you should consider purchasing a new dog bed that has sufficient cushioning to provide comfort to your dog or augmenting a current bed with padding. You may want to consider an alternate sleeping arrangement if your dog cannot sleep in his normal spot. For example, if your home has more than one story, consider the ability of your dog to walk up and down stairs in determining where he should sleep. If necessary, use baby gates to cordon off areas that might be dangerous for your dog if he were to fall or lose balance.

In my canine cancer experience, I felt very strongly about being near to my dog throughout the night. So, on those nights when he could not make the trip upstairs to bed, I chose to sleep on the couch downstairs with him instead. This occurred somewhat randomly; I could not find a correlation between his behavior and his ability to come upstairs. There were also nights that he could not make it up onto the couch; those nights, I slept on the floor next to him. I wanted to make sure that I was close by, so that I would know immediately if his condition had changed.

> When my son was six years old, he knew that if he woke in the middle of the night and I was not in my bedroom, that he should come downstairs and look for me there. It's amazing that such a young child was not fazed by the slight change of plans and the interruptions to our daily routines. He took it all in stride. I encourage you to include your children in the process of what is happening with your dog, as this will start to prepare them for what might lie ahead. Age appropriate discussions make the process less scary to a child.

Grooming

Through grooming our dogs, we are sending them a message that we care for and love them dearly and that they are worthy of our care. Most dogs love to be touched and held by their owners, and this will help them feel more grounded and cared for, even when they may not feel good or are in pain. So even if your dog is very sick, you should continue your regular home grooming routine with him, being careful of any parts of his body that might be painful because of the cancer. Grooming activities do not need to be time consuming.

Spending even ten to fifteen minutes per day will send a positive message of love and acceptance to your dog. These activities include:

- Bathing (a sponge bath can be a more relaxing and easier option).
- Brushing.
- Nail clipping.
- Ear cleaning.
- Teeth cleaning.

For dogs that have become incontinent, it is critical to keep their hind areas clean and dry so that bacteria do not have an opportunity to set in and cause an infection. This will require frequent monitoring on your part, as well as laundering of bed coverings. It may be helpful to purchase a waterproof mattress pad that you can place over your dog's bed and cover with a soft towel or blanket that can be easily washed if necessary. If you can, purchase two sets so that you can swap a dry set for a soiled set.

Keeping a positive and happy outlook

Most dog owners know how perceptive their dogs are to how they are feeling. It's important to keep a positive, happy outlook when around your dog so that he does not suffer undue anxiety from the stress of your feelings about his condition. Remember that dogs live in the present and do not think about what is to come in the future. They enjoy the current moment they are in fully, without giving a thought to what the next minute might bring. If you break time into durations of say ten minutes, ten days, and ten years, you can imagine where you and your dog will be at those points in time. It's safe to say that in ten minutes, you'll either be enjoying the same task you are now, or perhaps you'll have moved on to something else. Ten days could be a little tricky, based on the stage of where you are with your dog. You could be in exactly the same place as you are now, or things may have progressed for better or worse. Most likely, it's safe to say that in ten years, your dog will have passed on, and what you will have are all of the memories that you shared together.

So, since you know what the ultimate outcome will be, why fret over the details and worry? This only makes your dog more anxious and stressed. Try to let go of the specifics and focus instead on this very moment with your dog. Enjoy your time with him and love him with all of your heart. That is exactly what he is doing, too.

Massage and other body work

The last of the list of things to improve the quality of life for a dog with cancer is the use of massage. I will admit that I knew nothing about animal massage prior to my first canine cancer experience. It was my mom, to whom I am forever grateful, who stepped up to the challenge when my first dog was diagnosed with cancer. An avid reader and master of the local library system, she armed me with information to help in our battle with cancer. One of the things some books recommended was massage, so my mom read about and taught herself how to do dog massage and then showed me how to do it. I later incorporated other techniques such as acupressure and energy healing methods to help improve my dog's quality of life. Some form of massage then became a daily ritual that we enjoyed every day from that point forward. On bad days, I would massage him more than once, just to get my hands close to him so that he would know how much I loved him.

Since then, I have found many resources for animal massage that are included at the back of the book. I had the privilege to interview Lola Michelin, Director of Education and Founder of the Northwest School of Animal Massage, for this book. She recommends that you find a professional in your area who can perform an initial assessment of your dog, and then teach you some basic techniques that will be most appropriate for your dog's condition. If this is not possible, she suggests that you research techniques in books or videos, so that you can view a demo. The following guidelines should be used when incorporating animal massage into your routine:

- Intention is everything.
- Assess the health of your dog and accommodate any restrictions by avoiding areas that are painful or tender to the touch.
- Never massage if your dog has a fever or an infection.

- Let your dog guide the experience and duration; don't force it. Even ten minutes of massage or petting will provide benefits to your dog.

- If someone other than you is doing the massages, request that your dog be massaged at home, if possible, to create less stress.

- Let go of any expectations you might have about how your dog will react. Sometimes it takes a few sessions before he understands what is happening.

Megan Ayrault (see www.AllAboutAnimalMassage.com) has created several webinars and e-books that provide a good overview of the basics of animal massage. According to Megan, there are many benefits to animal massage, including how it:

- Assists the nervous system to go into "relaxation mode." Healing happens during relaxation, not during stress.

- Strengthens the immune system.

- Creates a deeper bond with you.

- Instills greater confidence as the enhanced communication it provides will help you know how your dog is feeling.

- Benefits the muscles, nerves, respiratory system, circulatory system, lymphatic system, skin, etc.

Proper massage techniques

Always use light pressure. There is a misconception that deep pressure is most effective, but this can actually cause bruising in your dog. To avoid this, use pressure like what you use when petting your dog or resting your hand on the dog's shoulder. Should your pet have a need for deep tissue massage, for example to work on scar tissue, then it is best to find a professional who can do this for you. Similarly, if your dog requires stretching exercises, this is another situation where a professional's help should be solicited. It's possible to do injury by stretching incorrectly. You can find a network of animal professionals at http://animalwellness.ning.com.

Depending on the treatment protocol that is being used, such as chemotherapy or radiation, you may want to consider massage 24 to 48 hours before the treatment. Massage will enhance circulation, which will allow the chemotherapy or radiation to more effectively reach all areas of the body. Wait 24 to 48 hours after treatments like chemotherapy or radiation. Your dog may also be more susceptible to bruising and can feel nauseated and grumpy immediately after treatments. By waiting the suggested time period, you will have better results.

After only three to five massages, your dog will let you know what he/she likes. It is helpful if you can establish a routine, with the following elements, so that your dog will learn to associate the massage with good feelings:

- Perform the massage at the same time of day.
- Set up in the same area of the same room.
- Use the same dog bed.
- Play the same CD, such as *Through a Dog's Ear* (http://www. throughadogsear.com/) or some other music or sounds that might be calming for your dog. According to Dr. Lisa Reising at the Animal Healing Center in Redmond, Washington, "harp music is very healing."

The Appendix has several resources that can help you get started with animal massage. The important thing to know is that you don't necessarily need to know anatomy or special techniques in order to evoke benefit from the massage for your dog. Benefits to all systems of the body will result simply because a healing response is triggered as your dog relaxes to your touch. Of course, it is important to take cues from our animals—if your dog is not enjoying the massage session, you'll know! In fact, Megan Ayrault notes that "animals get more communicative with their body language as you respond to their cues."

Other body work techniques

Simple energy healing. Mary Calanni of Big Mountain Wildlife Animal Sanctuary uses an energy healing technique to help her sick animals recover more quickly and fully. She passed this method on to me and it is as follows:

- Cradle your dog's head in your hands.

- As you breathe deeply, will the cancer from his body.

- Imagine that you are healing him through your breath and energy and hands.

To be honest, I'd never considered myself a healer before, and I never thought my hands were anything special, but I was willing to extend myself and try anything that might possibly help him. I'd look at him eye to eye and it seemed to me that he understood what was happening. (Note: this worked with my dog's personality, but each dog is different.) I don't know what might have happened had we not done these exercises, but in the end, it gave us a very special time to share that we both looked forward to every day.

Extended petting sessions. If you are not comfortable with trying animal massage techniques on your dog, consider gently petting him/her for ten minutes, every day. Focus on using long strokes that start at the head and go all the way along the back to the tip of the tail. This does not require any special skills, and yet it provides great benefits. As you slowly switch your attention and focus to your dog, you will be aiding circulation of blood and lymphatic fluid, which will act as a stimulus to the immune system. Dogs are kinesthetic learners, so they may move around while you are petting or massaging them. Even if they get up, they may come back and sit or lie down for more. But you should never perform petting sessions for longer than your dog is comfortable with.

Acupuncture. Acupuncture is used to balance the flow of Qi (energy), which has become stagnant in diseases such as cancer. It utilizes fine needles to reach specific points to release pain and tension and promote healing.

Acupressure. Acupressure is similar to acupuncture, except that finger pressure is used instead of needles to release pain and tension and promote healing. For example, Collene Gaolach of Northwest Animal Holistic Health suggests the use of the "Stomach 36" or "Leg Three Mile" acupoints to relieve gastrointestinal issues such as nausea, vomiting, diarrhea or constipation. With this technique, use either your thumb or middle finger supported on your pointer finger, to apply pressure at a 45 to 90 degree angle to your animal's body.

There are two acupoints located just to the outer side and below the animal's left and right knees. It may seem your animal has two boney knee projections—use the lower one. This acupoint is unlike other acupoints in that it is long and linear. It also stimulates the immune system. The only time it should not be used is with pregnant animals.

> With one of my dogs, I scheduled an acupuncture treatment every other week, and he always bounced back after the appointments. His appetite was better, he slept better and he was more mobile. With my other dog, my veterinarian recommended a treatment that incorporated homotoxicology, which in this instance involved taking a small blood sample, adding various homeopathic remedies, and injecting the mixture at appropriate acupuncture points. Note that not all homotoxicology treatments involve taking blood and performing injections. Due to the short duration of his treatment because of the rapid progression of his cancer, it's difficult to evaluate how this treatment plan affected him.

I've provided a variety of ways beyond nutrition and treatment that can make a difference in the quality of life that your dog enjoys during their battle with cancer. View this all as information that you can choose to adapt to your individual situations. The bottom line is that you need to do what is right for you, your dog, and your family, and what you can live with for what may be an extended period of time. Hospice care is a commitment that requires an abundance of your time and resources, but you can also use your creativity and ingenuity to develop unique solutions to your problems.

CHAPTER 7

Prevention

Having gone through two canine cancer experiences, I can assure you that you will want to do everything you can to prevent it from happening in the first place. While it would be wonderful to be able to say that if you followed a few simple rules your dog would never contract cancer, we all know that this is not realistic. One difficulty is that in many cases the cause of cancer is never determined. And even if you faithfully follow all the preventive measures in this chapter, there could still come a day that your dog contracts cancer. Or it could be that you did everything wrong, and somehow, your dog manages to live to a ripe old age, never succumbing to this scary disease. All you can do is to try to minimize the chances of cancer through prevention.

What we do know is that there are several contributing factors to cancer, some of which we can control and some of which we cannot. What we can do is try to manage the contributing factors and attempt to lessen the effect that any one of the have on our dogs. These factors include:

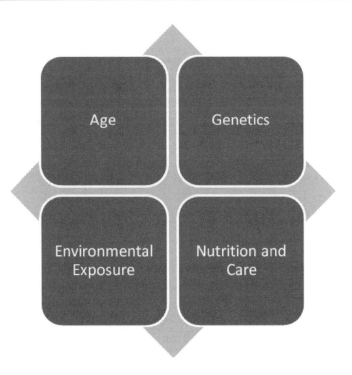

Age. As cells age, whether human or canine, they do not function as efficiently as they did when they were younger. Sometimes aging cells are not as able as they used to be to fend off attacks by foreign cells. Over time, cells may mutate with negative effects and the immune system may become compromised by other illnesses.

Genetics. Without knowing the full genetic line of your dog's parents, it can be impossible to tell if genetics will play a role in whether your dog will ever get cancer. Certain breeds are prone to specific types of cancer. Female dogs are more susceptible to mammary cancer than males, particularly if they are not spayed before their second heat.

Environmental exposure. This includes everything from exposure to the sun's rays to vicarious cigarette smoke to dangerous lawn chemicals. In the same way that prolonged sun exposure can cause skin cancer in humans, this can also happen in dogs. Use common sense when purchasing potentially toxic products for your home and lawn, and consider ways to reduce the chances of your dog coming into contact with these products. Both you and your dog will benefit.

Poor nutrition and care. What your dog eats, as well as the quality of the water he drinks, plays a huge role in ensuring that he has the building blocks necessary to promote strong, healthy cells, as well as a tough immune system. Question the source of everything that you feed your dog. Unless you are sure that the ingredients are wholesome, don't feed it to him. There are many books listed in the Appendix that you can use as a resource to learning how to feed your dog more natural and pure foods without having to spend large sums of money to do so.

Steps you can take
While it may be sobering to learn that there is no guaranteed method to prevent cancer, all is not lost. There are many actions that you can take to provide your dog with the maximum protection possible. Through all of my research, I have come to the conclusion that you can help to prevent the occurrence of cancer by following these rules:

Avoid environmental and household toxins. There are many harmful substances that can be found commonly in and around the home that may contribute to the incidence of cancer in our dogs, as well as in us. Deborah Straw, in her book *Why Is Cancer Killing Our Pets?* warns owners to be very careful about exposure to the following:

- Antifreeze.
- Household cleaning agents.
- Lead.
- Rodenticides.
- Flea products.
- Rawhide.
- Tobacco smoke.
- Golf courses (because of fertilizers and pesticides).
- Smoked dog food products (wood smoke can contain carcinogenic products).

- Plastic chew toys.

- Pig's ear and noses (can be processed with chemicals and dyes; especially do not purchase these from unmarked bins).

It is not possible to declare with certainty that particular substances will cause cancer in dogs. That said, there are studies that link exposure to lawn chemicals and strong magnetic fields to lymphoma and other cancer types, but there is no strong proof that this is the case. My suggestion, and what I have done in my own household, is to switch to as many natural or organic products as is practical and to use common sense regarding the use of chemicals and artificial substances in your home. Read *Slow Death by Rubber Duck: The Secret Danger of Everyday Things*, by Rick Smith and Bruce Lourie, a book that calls attention to the dangers that may currently exist in our own homes, many of which we believe are innocuous products. A rule I use is that if something is potentially dangerous for me, then it is also dangerous for my dogs.

Feed healthy and nutritious food. Recommendations for what to feed your dog and what supplements will help were made in Chapter 5. In Traditional Chinese Medicine, the theory is that there is a strong link between the foods that we eat and what happens in our bodies. Cancer is believed to be caused by eating improper food and toxins, which leads to the accumulation of phlegm (in the form of tumors) and the stagnation of Qi (energy) and blood in the body. Unfortunately some types of commercial dog food may have improper ingredients (including the remains of euthanized pets) and toxins according to Ann Martin in her book *Food Pets Die For*. I recommend you avoid most kinds of commercial dog food. Ann's book is sure to open your eyes to the horrors of the commercial pet food industry.

Provide your dog with access to clean, filtered water every day. Be sure to at least rinse out the bowl each day with hot water, and thoroughly clean it with hot, soapy water at least once per week. Stick with glass, stainless steel or stoneware bowls; avoid plastic.

Limit vaccines to those required by law and/or necessary to prevent serious disease. Ask your veterinarian about titering. This is a process by which a small amount of blood is taken from your dog and sent to a lab for analysis. A titer will determine the level of concentration of a particular antibody in your dog's blood, which will indicate whether additional vaccination is necessary or not. While this process is a little pricey ($98 in Washington state in 2009), the peace of mind in prevention is worth it.

Carefully research any medicines. Does your dog really need heartworm medicine? Flea medicine? The need for medicines like these is largely based on the region where you live. For example, here in Washington State, I do not use a preventive for either heartworm or fleas. In Colorado however, my dogs were on heartworm medicine for six months of the year. Check with your veterinarian as to the necessity of these medicines in your area. Inquire about natural alternatives that can be substituted instead. There are many natural flea remedies that you can find just by performing an internet search for "natural alternatives for flea prevention"

As an alternative to flea products, Dr. Martin Goldstein, DVM recommends that feeding garlic and Brewer's yeast to your dog will make him less palatable to fleas. You may also try sprinkling Brewer's yeast on your dog's coat.

Use natural fertilizers and weed killers. There are many organic fertilizer and weed killer products on the market today. Before I knew about the risks of these chemicals on dogs, I lived for a few years in a home located on a golf course. It never occurred to me that my property might be contaminated with the same toxic fertilizers and weed killers that were used on the golf course. I have always wondered if that was a contributing factor to my first dog's cancer.

Ensure your dog gets plenty of exercise, tailored to size and age. Take multiple walks per day, if possible. Run, swim, play fetch—any activity that your dog enjoys to keep him active and trim.

Consider a mutt. While it is not a guaranteed solution, mutts may have less genetic exposure to cancer. Inbreeding is a problem with some breeds and can perpetuate cancer between generations. Visit a local animal sanctuary or shelter and see if there is some wonderful, mixed breed dog who touches your heart.

Set aside time each month to thoroughly examine your dog for any unusual lumps or bumps, or changes in existing lumps or bumps. Make a note of anything you notice and be sure to let your veterinarian know. If your next appointment won't be for several months, call the office and leave a message for him/her, explaining what you observed and any additional concerns you may have. If the veterinarian suspects anything serious, he or she will let you know. If your gut tells you it's something serious, make an appointment.

Evaluate home screening kits that are now available. These early detection urinalysis test kits allow you to screen for many diseases before symptoms may occur. See http://www.thepetcheckup.com for more information.

Know your dog. Lastly, as I mentioned in Chapter 2, perhaps it is most important to observe your dog and keep a log of behaviors. Remember that regardless of how insignificant a symptom might seem—even excessive coughing or sneezing can be a sign of cancer—it is important to document its frequency and duration. The important thing is that you assess a baseline for your dog, and then monitor it on a regular basis. It's a good idea to purchase a notebook for every dog in your life, so that you can use it to record anything of note, including the results of any examinations that you perform. Sketch out the approximate outline of your dog, and then indicate the location of any abnormalities. You can also indicate the size of any fatty tumors or other growths, and do a recheck every one to two months to determine if there have been changes in size, shape, density, etc. Your veterinarian will appreciate this detailed note-taking should any health problems arise. In summary, the following signs can all be potential indicators of cancer, although each may also occur due to other illnesses:

- Unusual fatigue and/or weakness, with the extreme being lameness.
- Vomiting.
- Diarrhea.
- Discoloration in urine or stools.
- Bad breath.

- Rapidly growing masses.

- Excessive, unusual coughing and/or sneezing.

- Loss of appetite.

- Pain (note that many dogs are stoic when it comes to pain, so this might be difficult to assess).

- Changes in quality of skin and coat.

- Blindness.

- Seizures.

The overarching message is that it is very important to maintain a diary over time, to capture any changes in your dog's behavior or characteristics. In this way, you can keep track of and note potential correlations in your dog's behavior to other environmental factors that may be present in your dog's life at that time.

There is no panacea for preventing cancer, whether in dogs or humans. We can only do our best each and every day to live our lives and provide for our dogs in the best way we know how at any given moment. The famous poet Maya Angelou once said, "When you know better, you do better." This is sage advice for each and every one of us who thought we were providing the best for our dogs, only to realize years later that we were endangering our pets and ourselves in the process. You can't beat yourself up for something you didn't know. But you can ensure that it never happens again.

For me personally, you can bet I will never live on, or even near, a golf course ever again. That said, one of my other dogs, Scooby, the half-brother to Porter, also lived with us in that house on the golf course. He is now twelve and still in the best of health. Until just recently, we still ran three miles several times a week, and he continues to be an active swimmer and hiker with our family. So, it just goes to show that it's impossible to know with any certainty what impact we have; could it be entirely genetic? Nutritional? Environmental? At the end of the day, we can only do the best we can do at any given moment.

CHAPTER 8

The Natural Dying Process

You may or may not have had prior experiences with death. While many of us have attended wakes or funerals to honor those family members and friends who have passed on during our lifetimes, I think it's likely that few of us have actually been in the presence of a dying being. I know this was the case for me. I had only seen people and animals die in movies and on TV, so I was ill prepared for the real-life version. Keep in mind that every death experience is unique. While I will share with you a general progression through the natural dying process, note that each stage has a wide range of physical manifestations, as well as variations in duration. When I speak of natural death, what I mean is the process by which an animal passes of her own volition, in her own time. When an animal dies naturally, we do not take any action to either prolong her passing or hasten it; we merely offer support, by ensuring that she is able to rest comfortably via soft beds and pillows, that she is neither too hot nor too cold and that she is in a calm, quiet environment.

According to Tibetan Buddhism, there are eight stages of dying. The first four stages occur during what we Westerners would consider life, and the latter four stages occur after the final exhale from the body has occurred, during what we would consider death. These stages of dying provide a very nice construct within which to describe the progression towards death, and the way in which it is presented by the Tibetan Buddhists is so respectful of the natural processes that occur. When I learned of these stages of dying during the *Spirits in Transition* seminar, I was comforted by the sheer simplicity and matter-of-factness with which they were presented. It was only after learning about the process of dying under hospice care that I recognized several mistakes I made with my first dog with cancer. I took great care not to make these same mistakes twice once I learned what to expect and how to recognize each stage.

Here is a brief summary of the symptoms commonly observed throughout the stages of natural dying, and things one can do to offer support.

Stage 1

This stage can last days or weeks, during which a decline in the animal's habits and daily functions takes place. It is often characterized by the following:

- Possible loss of appetite, but may still be enticed by offering varying food choices.

- Weight loss (may have already started during senior years), due to loss of appetite above or despite eating well.

- Your dog may sleep longer, rest more and more, move less and less.

- Your dog will still go on walks.

- Gums, lips and tongue look pink and moist in healthy dogs. As the end is getting close the gums may turn white or grey.

- Toward the end of this phase, the dog will remain on his bed and his eyes may no longer close completely.

- Your dog's energy level decreases, as the body muscles are losing their strength and function.

What you can do:

- While your dog can still move about, consider what of his favorite things he may want to experience one more time, including what human and animal friends might want to come visit.

- Provide a variety of foods. Feed by hand if needed, but don't force feed him if you believe that this is the start of the dying process. (See sidebar below.)

- Provide a calm, quiet environment.

- If you notice that his eyes remain somewhat open during rest, ensure lights are dim and soothing, not bright.

- Promote comfort with supportive bed and pillows if needed for best positioning. Once your dog remains in his bed, if you feel he needs to be kept warm, use a heater rather than a blanket because a cover can now feel very heavy to the dog.

- Nurture your dog with comforting words. Once he just remains in resting position, if you feel he would like to be touched, use only very soft, slow petting strokes. It is important to be very gentle.

> *If your dog is uninterested in food, this does not in and of itself signal the start of the dying process. There are many causes for loss of appetite and you would not want to overlook treatable reasons, so make sure to consult with your veterinarian. Sometimes a loss of appetite is due to side effects of medications, meaning the treatment plan has to be changed. It could also be due to nausea, which can also be treated. Also see if changing the offered food may entice an animal to eat. Vary among foods of different smells, textures and temperature. When your dog first exhibits signs of diminished appetite, first try changing what you are offering, whether it is the ingredients (beef vs. lamb vs. chicken vs. egg), texture of food (hard vs. soft — try baby food), temperature (try warming the food a little), timing (maybe several smaller meals throughout the day are more palatable than a full breakfast and dinner only), mode of feeding (try hand feeding). In addition, watch for signs of nausea: the animal may show interest while you are preparing the food, but turn away after sniffing it. Or he may show excessive drooling or lip smacking, indicating nausea. Treat for nausea to see if it helps.*

Stage 2

This stage can last as long as days, or be as short as a few minutes. It is characterized by the following:

- Your dog's mouth may start feeling dry, urination may become less frequent.

- "Last bloom" may occur—your dog may move around or even eat or drink, when he had stopped doing this before.

- As his body continues to shut down its processes, water may no longer be desired, and bodily fluids start to dry up.

What you can do:

- Maintain a calm environment, with lights dim if eyes no longer close.

- Consider moistening your dog's lips and gums gently with lukewarm water if it seems welcomed by your dog, for instance by using a cotton swab.

- Begin any final preparations that you plan to make, as typically there are only 24 to 48 hours left after your dog stops drinking. This might include inviting family and close friends for a final visit, gathering extra blankets and towels, notifying your office that you will be unavailable, etc.

- Avoid forcing water intake at this stage. Once your dog won't drink from a bowl, offer water by syringe for as long as the dog willingly takes it in. If giving subcutaneous fluids are part of the recent treatment plan, amounts given need to be adjusted to the lessening ability of the body to absorb them, and at some point they should be discontinued. Otherwise they can start creating discomfort to your dog by causing edema, nausea, vomiting, even difficulty breathing. In short, forced drinking may become counter-productive to creating a peaceful dying process.

- Bring other family pets to see your dog so that they can see their buddy once more; you may want to invite other family members as well.

- Continue to keep towels or disposable incontinence pads under both the front and the back of your dog.

> *As your dog becomes dehydrated, pain medications he may have been on may now work at a lower dose. This also means the risk for side effects increases if the dose does not get adjusted, so seek your hospice veterinarian's input.*

Stage 3

Once your dog reaches this stage, there are usually only minutes left. It is characterized by the following:

- Body temperature may become colder, breath coming out of mouth may feel cool.

- Digestion ceases. There may be a last release of urine or a final bowel movement, although this can occur in stage 4 or later.

- Breathing may become shallower, with exhale more pronounced, less frequent breaths.

- Your dog no longer takes note of loved ones and surrounding environment as he is getting ready to depart.

- As the body progresses towards a natural death, his body can no longer maintain the temperature range normal throughout life.

What you can do:

- Speak softly to your dog and offer reassuring words.

- Hold or touch your dog very gently. If it feels right, respect the process that your dog is going through. Again, it is important to be very gentle at this stage.

- Gather your family members to provide support to your dog.

- Keep soft towels or disposable incontinence pads under both the front and the back of your dog.

> *Even with the knowledge of these stages, it can be difficult to remember everything when it is actually happening. It helps to have a friend or family member who can be counted on to remind you of what can be done at each stage. It also*

> *helps to have an "End Plan" that captures your last wishes for the end, that you can share with others who are there supporting you. See the example at the back of the book. When Jasper was dying, I was so immersed in the process that was ongoing with him that I neglected to put some blankets under his hind end, even though they were only three feet away from me. When a huge release of fluid came out of him, I realized what I had forgotten. A portable carpet cleaner is very useful on such occasions.*

Stage 4

This stage occurs rapidly, often lasting only few minutes. It is characterized by the following:

- Eye movements are slowed.
- Dog is hardly aware of surrounding environment.
- Breathing might get infrequent.
- Involuntary twitching of limbs may occur.
- Arching of neck or stretching out of limbs may occur.
- Howling or moaning sounds may be made.
- Final fluid release such as urination may occur, or a last bowel movement.
- Final exhale occurs.
- This marks the end of the physical dying process.

What you can do:

- Be quiet and still, reserve crying as much as possible until the process is over so you can offer a loving farewell to your beloved dog.
- A release of fluids from the bladder, anus, mouth or nose may occur sometime after the final breath, so make sure to continue to keep clean towels or fluid absorbent pads under both the head and the hind end. The fluids may contain some blood too.

Again, remember there are many variations possible during the natural death process. You may only notice a few of the listed signs of your animal going through this process or you may find that the timing occurs much faster. Your dog may continue to eat all the way up until his last day, for example. Each process is individual, yet it may help you, as it helped me, to understand some of the common occurrences.

After physical death

There is no need for any rush once your dog has passed; no immediate action has to be taken. You can take some time to process, reminisce and listen: what do you sense in the silence that remains after that last breath?

There are many cultures and religions that believe that the spirit of the deceased stays in the body for three days after death, which is why many traditions involve wakes, viewings, etc. in the first few days after death. In Tibetan Buddhism, stages 5 to 8 are believed to occur during the first few days after death, and are thought to include releasing ordinary mind states such as feelings of sorrow, fear, hunger, thirst and then more subtle mind states. Whatever your belief, it is your decision to act in whatever way works for you, your family and your belief system. If you choose to wait some time prior to burial or cremation, you may consider ahead of time how you will contain the body and any remaining fluids. You may want to use bags of crushed ice to keep the body cold, in order to delay the process of decomposition and keep scents down. You may feel compelled to decorate the area your dog is in with candles, flowers and any other meaningful items. Those who have loved your dog may appreciate being offered to see him once more even now. Be sure to explain the process to any children, as this might be frightening to them.

Burial, cremation and memorials

Hopefully, you have considered the options of burial and cremation and know your preferences ahead of time. Many veterinary clinics will allow you to bring your pet to their office and they will arrange for cremation. If you choose this route, be sure to specify whether you prefer that your dog be cremated alone or with other pets. Some facilities will cremate more than one pet at a time, and divide the ashes accordingly, which helps to minimize cost.

In addition, there are now companies in many regions that will arrange for pickup of your dog, as well as cremation or burial. For example, David Haarsager, owner of Heartfelt Memories in Seattle, Washington will provide these services, and can also recommend ways to memorialize your dog.

> It helps to think about your opinions and feelings regarding potentially difficult topics, such as autopsies, extent of resuscitation, euthanasia, and care of the body. It's better to think about this before you are faced with a time-bounded question, so that you are not influenced by circumstances in the moment.

CHAPTER 9
Embracing Grief and Honoring Memories

"Grief comes from trying to protect anything from being what it is. From trying to stop the change." - Stephen Levine, 1982

Regardless of how well we have cared for our beloved dogs and how much we loved them, there will come the day that remains forever etched in our hearts as the one where they breathed their last breath. If the battle with cancer was long and difficult, you may feel a sense of relief that your dog is no longer suffering and is finally at peace. If the battle was short, you may still be in shock at the speed with which this day arrived. Whatever the particulars of your situation, you can trust that it was unique and profound. It will take time for you to process what happened and proceed through some or all of the steps of the grieving process. Dr. Elisabeth Kubler-Ross was the first to introduce five stages of grief in her book *On Death and Dying*. In her model, the five stages are:

- Denial
- Anger
- Bargaining
- Depression
- Acceptance

Not everyone will experience each stage, and the stages will not necessarily occur in the order listed. However, as you process the grief and mourn the loss of your beloved pet, you will experience a wide range of emotions and thoughts. Above all, as you grieve, be kind to yourself. Allow yourself the time and space to properly mourn your loss. Remember that the process of grief is different for each individual, so you should neither rush, nor feel guilty about taking the time you need to get through your grief. Honor your own unique process. Read books or listen to audio books to help you through your loss, such as:

- *Dogwood and Catnip: Living Tributes to Pets We Have Loved and Lost*, Marsha Olson, Fairview Press, Minneapolis, Minnesota, 2003.
- *Tuesdays with Morrie*, Mitch Albom, Doubleday, New York, New York, 1997.
- *Honoring the Journey: A Guided Path Through Pet Loss*, KaLee R. Pasek, DVM, Self-published, 2008.
- *All Pets Go To Heaven*, Sylvia Browne, Fireside, New York, New York, 2008.
- *28 Days of Grief and Healing—Transforming the Loss of a Beloved Animal Companion*, Claire Chew, MA, Citysound Music, Venice, California, 2011.

If you need to talk to someone or seek therapy, do so. Grieving the loss of a pet is a very difficult thing. When I was grieving the loss of my first dog to cancer, someone told me that it would get better over time, and that I would eventually come to a place where I would find comfort and happiness in the memories of our lives together. It is true that grief subsides over time, but I don't necessarily believe that it ever fully goes away. As we move towards the stage of acceptance, the overwhelming and intense emotions that we felt initially are often replaced by sadness, loneliness, or the feeling that there is something missing.

There are many hotlines available. Use your favorite search engine to search for "pet grief hotline" and you may be surprised at the many resources available to you. Registered Psychologist Jean Griffin compiles a thorough list at her site, http://www. petloss.com/phones. htm. Be aware that not all support lines are created equal; check the appendix for specific notes on each support line that I was able to contact.

Most support lines are offered through veterinary colleges and have a limited set of hours, typically a few hours in the evenings that are staffed by veterinary students. These students have received training—two hours seemed to be the average length—consisting of seminars, videos and role playing in how to work with people who have just experienced the loss of their pet. The typical phone call lasts anywhere from 20 to 60 minutes, and the volunteers are encouraged to listen and then assist the caller with identifying ways to handle his or her grief by suggesting additional resources available to the public. Callers are encouraged to call back for additional support, if needed; there is no limit in most cases. All offer to send a packet of follow-up information with additional resources, websites and sometimes a listing of local support groups and therapists that the callers can contact for more assistance. If callers phone outside of the normal support line hours, they are able to leave a message and can expect a timely call back.

A standout among these support lines is the help line offered by the University of Tennessee, College of Veterinary Medicine, started in 2002 by Dr. Elizabeth Strand, DVM. This help line is available Monday through Friday, from 9 am to 6 pm Eastern Time and is staffed by social work professionals, who are either masters-level social workers or masters-level social work interns. In addition, each caller is offered four free one-hour grief counseling sessions. Sarina Lyall, LMSW, has answered calls on this help line since her internship in 2008 and has been full time since 2009. She recognizes that when she speaks with a pet owner who has lost a beloved animal, it is often the first time that the caller has reached out for help in dealing with the loss of the pet. "The relationship with our animals is so profound," she adds. "We try to help people remember the good times and celebrate their animal's life, instead of focusing on death."

It is worth thinking about what you are looking for from a support line. Do you just want someone to listen to your story? Or would you prefer professional counseling? Or do you need a list of internet resources and a list of books to read? Once you know what you are looking for (or even if you don't), I encourage you to read about the support lines I have included in the Appendix and pick a few to call. I'd also recommend that you find a support line closest to where you live, in case there are local, in-person support groups that you can visit. A unique set of services is offered by Enid Traisman at the Dove Lewis Emergency Animal Hospital in Portland, Oregon. She provides a free one-hour pet loss support group four times each month, in addition to a free memorial arts therapy session on the second Sunday of every month. Each month's project is different and materials are provided for attendees.

There are many ways that you can memorialize your dog, and this can be somewhat therapeutic as you are progressing through the grieving process. Here are some unusual and interesting ways to honor the memory of your dog that I have discovered on various websites, through friends who have experienced the loss of a dog, and by my own quest to find a way to keep the memories strong.

Whether you choose to bury or cremate, you can consider having a special headstone created, or finding a special urn or box for ashes. If your county/city permits you to bury your dog on your property, you can plant a special tree, bush, or flowers to mark the area. An article in *The Seattle Times* entitled "Spending eternity with your pet" talks about a growing trend in America where pet owners want to be buried with their pets, and are reserving plots in pet cemeteries and leaving this wish in their wills. For more information about pet cemeteries and which accept human remains as well, you can visit the website of the International Association of Pet Cemeteries and Crematories at http://www.iaopc.com/who-are-we.

If your dog had a favorite spot on your property, you can choose to dedicate it to your dog, and erect a memorial of your design and/or special plantings. A friend in Seattle shared a special totem pole that was created when a family member's dog died:

You can also choose to memorialize your pet online as well, with the option to upload photos, video, audio, etc. Many of these sites are free, some charge fees after a trial period. A sampling of sites is listed below:

- www.rainbowbridge.com
- www.ilovedmypet.com
- www.critters.com
- www.immortalpets.com
- www.peternity.com/memorial-gallery
- www.petmemorial.com.

While your dog is still healthy, I suggest the following:

- Take a video of your dog in his favorite spot.
- Take lots of pictures of your dog and each family member.

- Snip off a lock of hair.

- Purchase a plaster kit from a crafts store so that you can take a paw print.

- Consider hiring an artist to draw or paint your dog.

- Create a plan for how you want to approach post-mortem activities, such as whether to cremate or bury, and how to memorialize your dog.

There are many sites that offer ways to memorialize your dog. Some unusual examples are:

- Pet prayer flags. The Tibetans believe that as the images fade from the flags through exposure to the elements, they become a permanent part of the universe, forever memorializing your dog, www.praysersonthewind.com.

- Art glass. A handcrafted piece of art glass containing some of your dog's ashes can be created per your specifications, www.artfromashes.com.

- White dove release. A white dove release can be part of a memorial service for your pet, and these professionals ensure that the doves are treated humanely, www.white-dove-releases.com/.

- Launch into deep space, orbit or lunar surface. Cremains are placed into an individual flight capsule and launched, www.celestis.com.

You can search the internet on "ways to memorialize my pet" or "memorialize your dog" and you will find many more creative ways to preserve your memories together.

When the time is right for you, you can create a scrapbook that contains pictures and other memorabilia that are special to you. Or create a DVD montage with photos and video footage that you can arrange with music. On each anniversary of your dog's death, you can visit your dog's favorite places and throw some ashes, or visit the spot where he is buried and meditate. At the end of the day, it is up to you to decide what feels right to you and how you should preserve your memories.

CHAPTER 10

Real-Life Canine Cancer Experiences

This chapter includes a number of real-life stories from people who have experienced cancer with their beloved dog. Each case is different, the outcomes are different and they are meant to illustrate the vast continuum of canine cancer experiences. There are common cancers and more rare cancers, and the decisions that need to be made are not always simple or easy. There is often not a "best" choice, but rather a choice that we make with the knowledge and understanding available to us at a given point in time. Remind yourself that hindsight is 20/20, and focus instead on how to treat and care for your dog in a way that minimizes his pain and discomfort and maximizes his ability to enjoy life. Sometimes what is best for our dog is the hardest choice for us, yet the people in these stories illustrate that making hard choices is often necessary when you are facing canine cancer.

If anything, what I want you to glean from these stories is that each and every experience you have with canine cancer will be unique. And how each of us chooses to deal with the diagnosis of cancer is unique. No veterinarian, no book, no friend can tell you how to treat your best friend; follow your heart and prove to him that you are worthy of his devotion.

Boomer and Carol

Born in September 1995, Boomer was a Christmas gift for Carol. Boomer, a lively little Tibetan Terrier puppy was three months old when he came to their home in North Texas. He was always in good health and stayed quite active through lots of exercise his whole life.

If anything, he had trouble gaining weight, as he was always very active. When he was eleven, in December 2006, Carol first noticed a funny little cough as they were traveling between New Mexico and Texas by car. She took him to the veterinarian in January for his annual examination, vaccinations and blood work to determine if there was a possible infection causing his cough; everything came back fine. The veterinarian prescribed some cough medicine. When the coughing didn't subside after a ten day course of the medication, she took him back to the veterinarian so that they could do further examination. After two more weeks and more medication, the veterinarian took some X-rays. This time, the veterinarian could hear something in his chest. Because the veterinarian was not sure of the diagnosis, he asked Carol for her permission to send the X-rays on to a special diagnostic clinic in Dallas. Four days later, Carol got a call from the veterinarian informing her that it was lung cancer. The X-rays showed little white spots all over both lungs, and indicated that the cancer had also spread throughout the rest of his body.

At this point, Carol was offered two choices: she could treat aggressively with chemotherapy or let the cancer take its course. Her veterinarian did not recommend chemotherapy because the cancer had already metastasized. Because of this, the cancer could not be eliminated, and treatment would perhaps only extend Boomer's life by two months. She chose to keep him as comfortable as possible, although there was no way to know how long this period would last. With everything she could learn about cancer and considering the lifespan of the breed (about thirteen years), she decided to do whatever they could do to ensure that he was comfortable and not in pain.

At this point, Boomer was still going for walks in the park, although he was showing signs of slowing down, and would often sit. Her son returned home from another part of Texas to be there with them and offer his support. At this point, Carol started to monitor Boomer constantly, and noticed immediately when he stopped eating. She switched his diet from dog kibble and prepared special meals of rice and hamburger meat, which he did eat. Then eventually, she switched to rice and lamb meat. Sometime later, he finally stopped eating altogether. There were also occasions where Carol would have trouble finding him, as he had a doggie door and would go outside for long periods of time. Each time, she would go outside and find him. Throughout this period, they would still take walks to the park, but he walked very slowly and then wouldn't move most of the rest of the day.

Because Carol had a close relationship with her veterinarian, she had his cell phone number, and was told to call if she were ever concerned that Boomer was in pain. That gave Carol some peace of mind that she had someone to reach out to if anything happened. By the end of February, Boomer had had nothing to eat or drink for three days and had lost over 40% of his body weight. He was so weak that he was sometimes unable to even stand. Knowing instinctively that he was reaching the end, she decided to take him for one last walk in the park. Then she and her husband took him to the veterinarian and he was euthanized. They stayed with Boomer to the end, and had a few moments alone with him. Afterwards, he was cremated and his ashes are now in a special box with his name on it. Carol plans to spread his ashes in the backyard and over their favorite trail, but has not been able to do this yet. To this day, she keeps a lock of Boomer's hair and his collar in remembrance as well.

Kess and Tombi

In November 2003, Kess was adopted from the Whatcom County Humane Society in Washington at around six months of age. The only health issue she experienced was periodic episodes of demodectic mange, which was treated with a topical cream. At around age two, she began to have some recurring lameness in her right hind leg. At first, Tombi assumed it was due to an injury from Kess's involvement in dog sports—at the time, she was involved in flyball. Tombi thought maybe she had pulled a muscle, so she gave Kess plenty of rest and kept her as still as possible, and the lameness eventually went away. This happened several times over the course of many years, but each time this happened there was never any swelling, and X-rays did not reveal that anything was awry. One day in the backyard while playing fetch, Kess went full-speed into the shed and began limping once more. After a few days when she seemed better, Tombi took her out to play and she collapsed. A trip to the veterinarian and an X-ray revealed that she had a ruptured disc over her hips. Kess was put on crate confinement and steroids for three months to see if it would heal on its own. After waiting all these months, Kess was allowed to go on leash walks or for short romps, but was not allowed to play with balls or catch discs. After a year of this level of restriction, she was allowed to run again. After all this time, Tombi had watched Kess's muscles atrophy and became frustrated and depressed that she was so restricted from movement.

After a few weeks of free range, Tombi noticed that Kess's ankle was quite swollen and was limiting her use of that leg. Her vet discovered a mass in the leg and, although the needle biopsy came back negative for cancer, the mass was still removed. The surgeon called after the surgery and was convinced that the mass was cancerous, but again, the test results came back negative for cancer. The leg remained swollen and never seemed to heal in spite of antibiotics and steroids that were administered. Tombi went to get a second opinion and this veterinarian suggested a compression wrap for twenty minutes at a time for several weeks. This required a forty minute drive each way and required that Kess be kept for the full day. This resulted in no improvement. So Tombi decided to get a third opinion and went to a local veterinarian specialty clinic, where they based their treatment on the fact that prior test results had come back negative for cancer. At this point, her leg just had not healed properly and no one could figure out why.

As the veterinarian began to review the options, Tombi interrupted and inquired if it was an option to simply amputate the leg since Kess was not able to use it anyway, and it was obviously causing discomfort. The veterinarian was relieved that Tombi raised this point, as most owners find this a very difficult conversation to have. Kess had surgery on 10/28/10, and her right hind leg was removed. Because all of the results had come back negative for cancer, Tombi declined the expense of testing yet again. The veterinary surgeon, however, was highly suspicious and curious and so performed a pathology exam on the amputated leg. What she discovered was a tumor that ran the full length of Kess's leg. She suspected it was cancer and asked Tombi's permission to

get it tested; Tombi agreed. The result was indeed cancer, a rare kind called synovial cell sarcoma. When this was determined, Kess was X-rayed to ensure that the tumor had not spread. As it turns out, amputation is the normal course of treatment for this kind of cancer, so Tombi had instinctively done the right thing. The whole process cost her family about $6,000.

What is curious about this case is that the test results came back negative for cancer every time until the final sample was submitted. What Tombi later learned was that not all testing facilities are created equal, and that the facilities used initially by her veterinarian were not as reliable as the ones used by the specialty clinic.

Luckily, recovery from amputation can be very quick in dogs, particularly for hind leg amputations, as in Kess's case. The first two weeks of recovery were the hardest, as Kess required various medicines every three hours (Gabapentin, Metacam and Tramadol) for pain and antibiotics to prevent infection. She spent the first night after surgery in the hospital, and Tombi slept by her side in an X-pen for the first two weeks. Since Tombi knew that Kess would only be able to lie down on one side for several weeks after the surgery, she invested in a soft pad and an orthopedic bed to ensure Kess would be comfortable. Kess also received daily rub downs on the side she could lie on to keep her from getting stiff.

After three to four days, Kess was already able to trot around. Two weeks after the surgery, she was outside playing in the snow, at four weeks she was running, and by eight weeks, she was able to do sports again. Kess and Tombi are actively involved in disc sports through the Washington Owners of Flying Disc Dogs (http://www. woofd2.com). Tombi felt that the pain management was excellent using these three combined medications. Kess was very drowsy from the medications the first five days, but became more active as she was then weaned off the different painkillers. Tombi made sure that she was extremely diligent about administering the medications on schedule.

For follow-up, the veterinarian recommended that Kess have X-rays every year. This is just a precaution, as this particular type of cancer has an extremely high cure rate after amputation. Tombi feels they were very lucky. Once she knew that Kess had cancer and started researching on the internet, she learned some very grim statistics about this type of cancer and realized how lucky they were. Kess is now also doing agility courses, as well as continuing to compete in Frisbee and performing demos at dog events. She went from not being able to run well for a few years to being able to do her sports only four weeks after surgery. At the time of the writing of this book, Kess had just been named the number two disc dog in Washington State with two second place finishes and one third place finish at a recent state championship. Go Kess! You can watch her one-year anniversary video here: http://www.youtube.com/watch?v=PXN7T7oxj3M.

Banner and Barb

Star Spangled Banner, aka "Banner," was born on July 1, 2002 in Monroe, Washington. The entire litter of Golden Retriever puppies was named using a Fourth of July theme per the breeder's request. Banner was a very healthy pup and went home with Barb at two months of age. He did not have any medical issues until he began to swallow rocks at age three. He wound up having surgery twice to remove the swallowed rocks. At around age five, he tore an ACL and had surgery to repair it. The following year, he had a gingivectomy, an operation which removes excess gingival tissue in the mouth.

It was not until January of 2011 that Barb noticed Banner's lip seemed to be raised up near his front teeth. She thought that maybe it was swollen because he had been bitten or stung by an insect. She tried to wait it out to see if it improved, but it only got worse and started to bleed, to the point of dripping. When Barb took him to the veterinarian, the veterinarian wasn't sure what was causing the condition, but said that his front top teeth needed to be removed because they were dying. After the teeth were removed, an X-ray was taken, which revealed a lump. They took a tissue sample, but it did not come back as cancer. The vet put him on an anti-inflammatory drug, Rimadyl, and antibiotics. There was less bleeding after the teeth were removed. An X-ray revealed that the tumor was isolated in the bone itself and had not spread to other nearby organs, such as the brain.

> Maxillary fibrosarcoma is a difficult cancer to diagnose, because the cancer grows in layers. In addition, in Banner's case, the fact that it was present in the front of the mouth was highly unusual. This type of cancer usually occurs in the back of the mouth.

Before Barb did anything further, she decided to get a second opinion and took Banner to a local veterinarian specialist clinic. In addition to specialist veterinarians, they also had a dental surgeon on staff. Both performed an examination, and had a high suspicion that it was cancer. By this time, it was late February 2011 and Barb made an appointment with a local oncologist to understand their options.

The news from the oncologist was grim. Essentially, with or without treatment, the oncologist provided a prognosis of two to six months. Barb did not have a good experience with this specialist, finding his office sterile and his demeanor unpleasant. He did tell her that he sees more Golden Retrievers over the age of seven with cancer than any other breed, and that 50 percent of Goldens eventually contract some form of cancer. In terms of options to treat the maxillary fibrosarcoma, the option with highest success rate was surgery, but due to the location of the tumor half of Banner's face would have been removed and he would have required some extensive reconstructive surgery afterwards. Another option would be to try either radiation or chemotherapy in lieu of surgery.

Before making a decision, Barb decided to get a second opinion from another oncologist. While this oncologist also shared the same prognosis of two to six months, she offered Barb the option of doing drip therapy (pamidronate) that would help to strengthen Banner's bones by reducing calcium loss and would also reduce pain. She discussed the option of radiation, but after learning that it could burn nearby sensitive tissue in his nose and possibly cause more pain, Barb decided against it. They also considered traditional chemotherapy, but ultimately, Barb decided against it because it had the potential for hair loss and other discomforts. Instead, she opted for Palladia and the results were great initially. The tumor shrank significantly. Their visits were once per week at first, so that blood test could be performed to verify liver function and also ensure that the dosages of medication were correct.

The Palladia was administered by Barb every other day, alternating days with prednisone, a steroid. Before giving the Palladia, Barb gave Banner Prilosec (to reduce acid) and ondansetron (to control nausea) an hour prior. Every three weeks, Banner went in for drip therapy, and would stay the entire day for the treatment. He was also taking Tramadol for pain management. Over the Memorial Day weekend, Banner had a very difficult time and almost died. He experienced diarrhea and extreme lethargy, didn't eat for two days straight, and drank little water. Barb's daughter was able to coax him into eating a little. (Something like this had happened previously, but was not of this severity or duration. At the time, she had given him mirtazaprine, used as an appetite stimulant, which did help.)

Barb decided that the treatments and medicines were just putting too much strain on Banner's body and she stopped the Palladia treatments, as the tumor had begun to grow again. At the time of our interview, Banner had been off Palladia and all other drugs for over a month. In spite of considerable growth of the tumor, Banner continued to be a very happy and active dog, never giving any indication that he was in pain or discomfort. The tumor became large enough that it pushed his nose up and out, so much so that he could no longer close his mouth. Occasionally, his jaw would bleed and he

experienced some minor difficulties with eating. Barb used the Chinese herb, Yunnan Baiyai, to help combat the bleeding.

Her oncologist told her about a new experimental drug for dogs with cancer, but Barb had already decided that she would not put Banner through extensive treatments again. Barb observed that Banner was a different dog when he was taking all of the medications, and noticed that he was much more himself, as well as both happier and healthier, without them. Banner was able to celebrate his ninth birthday at home, with special birthday cake and treats.

At the end of the summer, in late August, Barb and her family decided that Banner had been through enough, after more frequent bleeding episodes, difficulties eating and many bad days. She scheduled an in-home euthanasia, and the entire family was there with Banner through to the end.

Barb's advice to anyone facing canine cancer is to arm yourself with a list of questions to ask your veterinarian or other specialist and then to take lots of notes so that you can remember everything that was discussed. And if you don't like what one practitioner tells you, go get a second opinion. Looking back on her experience now, she remembers how confused she was about what care option to choose. She also felt the weight of Banner's comfort on her shoulders and how she wanted to make the right decisions.

Nelson and Jane

Nelson Lake, an Australian Shepherd/Border Collie mix, was four months old when Jane met him in February of 2001 through Echo Glen Canine Connections, a therapeutic program that aims to pair children in a correctional facility with dogs who need homes. Nelson had a horrible mange problem when Jane first brought him home, but she gradually corrected that condition and focused on training her mischievous pup, who wanted to play non-stop. Eventually, their training paid off and Jane and Nelson became registered Pet Partners with the Delta Society; the pair visited local nursing home patients on a regular basis.

In February 2008, Nelson was diagnosed with hip dysplasia. Tests taken at the time also revealed that he had low blood sugar. (While Jane feels that it must be somehow related to cancer, no medical professional could determine the cause. Ultimately, his blood sugar returned to normal.) Although Nelson was born with the hip dysplasia, it didn't become apparent until a cold, wet, February day when he and Jane played too much Frisbee and he had a hard time walking afterwards. At that point, Nelson started a regimen of hydrotherapy, acupuncture and hip stretching exercises. In April 2009, Nelson underwent stem cell therapy, which included harvesting belly fat, separating the stem cells and then inserting them into the hip joints to promote new bone and tendon growth to support his hips. This did improve the lameness related to the hip dysplasia.

In the summer of 2009, Jane recalls that Nelson developed a weird skin condition on his stomach that the veterinarians could not seem to diagnose. Working with her veterinarian, she gave Nelson antibiotics and prednisone to see if that would help. In December, she noticed a patch of missing fur near his neck, and soon after she felt a lump on his neck. In early January, Jane felt another lump on Nelson's neck. The lump was biopsied, and on January 12, 2010, Nelson was diagnosed with stage 1 lymphoma.

When Jane learned the news, she was overwhelmed. Her veterinarian referred her to an oncologist, and she learned that chemotherapy is very effective for lymphoma, especially in the early stages. She learned about the Madison Wisconsin Protocol, a six month chemotherapy program for lymphoma that has a success rate of 91 percent.[1] The protocol includes a mix of chemotherapy drugs including vincristine, doxorubicin, cyclophosphamide, and/or 1-asparagnase that are administered via an IV. Jane remembers that the program started out with weekly visits, then bi-weekly visits, leading up to longer intervals as the treatments progressed. The expected cost of this treatment was $4-5,000. Roughly 10 percent of the dogs who receive this protocol have a negative reaction to it. Unfortunately, Nelson fell in that 10 percent. As a result he had to be hospitalized a number of times and ultimately, his treatment cost skyrocketed to $10,000 because of his additional care needs.

[1] Dr. Mike Richards, DVM, http://www.vetinfo.com/dlymphoma.html, 3/18/99

The only complication was that because Nelson was part Australian Shepard, the oncologist had to perform a test to determine if he had the MDR1 gene mutation, which makes certain dogs sensitive to drugs, and causes a build-up of the drug in the patient's brain over time, ultimately causing severe neurological illness or even death. It took two weeks to get the test results back, so in the meantime Jane proceeded with the chemotherapy treatments, but at a much milder dosage than normally prescribed. The good news is that Nelson went into remission the week after his first treatment, on January 22, 2010. And he and Jane have not looked back since. Even though the average remission time is one year, Nelson has now been in remission over 25 months and counting.

As part of her approach to Nelson's care, Jane gathered a team of experts to help her: Western and holistic veterinarians, an oncologist, nutritionist, a physical/aquatic therapist and a pet sitter (also a veterinary technician), that allowed Jane to get a brief break when needed. She used the power of positive thinking and believed in the goodness of people's hearts as she and Nelson embarked on their journey to combat the cancer. During his treatment, she leveraged the expertise of each member of her cancer care team, and they found a balance of supplements that would support his immune and digestive systems while he was undergoing chemotherapy. Nelson took L-glutamine, an amino acid with healing properties; probiotics, for support of the digestive system; Cerenia to combat nausea; and Quercenase, an antioxidant that supports the gastrointestinal, respiratory and cardiovascular systems. He also received physical therapy and acupuncture treatments to counteract his nausea.

The experience led her to become more interested in what Nelson ate, and she learned about the benefits of high quality, grain-free food and the power of supplements. Nelson is now on a regimen of probiotics, salmon oil, liquid glucosamine, Protandim (an antioxidant), and Standard Process Canine Whole Body Support, and he eats a strictly grain-free diet. Nelson has a monthly vet visit to check for swollen lymph nodes and every third month this includes an abdominal scan and a blood test to ensure that there is no lymphoma in any of his organs and that everything is functioning well. At every visit, the reports show that Nelson is in amazing health and that his organs have stopped aging. Jane reports that he has never been healthier or looked better in his life, and recalls that his issues with chronic diarrhea are a thing of the past.

Throughout his life, Nelson received the standard vaccinations recommended by their veterinarian. Jane recalls that Nelson did spend many of his early years outside in the back yard, which was fertilized regularly by a yard service, and wonders if that could have been a causal factor in Nelson's lymphoma. She also wonders about the perennial tennis ball that Nelson would carry in his mouth and whether that could also have had an effect. However, the important element of Nelson and Jane's story is that it hasn't ended. Nelson is living a full life, free of cancer, and shows no sign of stopping.

Sora and Michelle

Sora was a European Boxer that Michelle brought over from Hungary. She was born in August 2000 and was about one and a half when Michelle took her home. While not entirely sure of her upbringing in Hungary, Michelle suspected that Sora did not have a good life initially and had been frequently confined. With respect to her medical history, she had some respiratory issues that were exacerbated with eating or activity and became easily overheated. At age three, Sora developed a limp, which might have been an ACL tear. By age eight, her ACL blew out and she required surgery. By this time, she also had some hip dysplasia and arthritis in her knee. Michelle wishes that she had had more knowledge around caring for a senior dog with orthopedic issues as she believes that this helped to weaken her immune system.

Sora had her first seizure about four months prior to her cancer diagnosis of canine insulinoma (a tumor in the pancreas). The second seizure came four months later and was much more serious than the first. She was taken to the emergency specialty veterinary clinic and kept overnight to run tests to determine the cause. The veterinarians wanted to put her on prednisone, but because she was already on an NSAID, they had to wean her off that first. The clinic felt that prednisone would be a good candidate to both stabilize her condition and her blood sugars, and prevent additional seizures. They felt that if the prednisone had a very positive effect, this might eliminate the need for surgery. Unfortunately, the prednisone did not have a significant effect, so Michelle and family opted for surgery, which offered them a chance to buy some time to figure out what to do next. At that point, if they had taken her home, they were told she would die.

Initially after the surgery to remove the tumor on July 5, 2010, the surgeon thought Sora's situation looked good, but a subsequent lab test revealed the presence of malignant cells. Michelle had a sinking feeling at that news—she had always taken such good care of her dogs and was devastated that in spite of that, Sora had cancer. At that point, her options were quite limited. The important task from then on would be to ensure that Sora did not have another hypoglycemic episode. If she did, the clinic recommended that she feed Sora some Karo corn syrup. At some point, they told Michelle that she would need to put Sora on prednisone to control the episodes.

Michelle went home, did lots of research on the internet, and joined a Yahoo! group called "Insulinoma Dogs." As she followed people's journeys with their dogs, she learned a lot and gained background on caring for canine insulinoma patients. When Sora's blood sugar became unstable, with symptoms of panting, anxiety, pacing and disorientation, Michelle started the prednisone in September, 2010. Although she knew that the medication caused an increased appetite, Michelle did not receive any guidance from the clinic regarding how to feed a dog who is taking prednisone. Sora's appetite was very strong, and she wound up gaining a lot of weight. She was also puffy from fluid retention. Part of the reason that Michelle fed her frequently was to keep her blood sugar stable, with the impression that "all cancer patients eventually waste away." While that might be the case with some cancers, it happens less often with insulinoma; this was a fact she learned after it was too late to return Sora to a healthy weight. Michelle asked many but no one had the answer: how do you help a dog lose weight if exercise pushed her into a hypoglycemic episode and she had to be fed five to six times a day???

Michelle consulted with Sora's holistic veterinarian, and discussed her ideas for how to help Sora. The holistic veterinarian was receptive to the ideas that Michelle had and willing to work with her to try various options, including acupuncture and herbs. By November of 2010, Michelle had enlisted a team of people who were available to assist, ranging from family to friends to skilled pet sitters and veterinarians.

Unfortunately, once Sora started to gain weight, everything became more difficult. She was more uncomfortable and had less energy. Since then, Michelle has suffered from the guilt of feeling that she let her dog get fat. As the dosage of prednisone increased for Sora, her working temperament caused her to become more anxious. Michelle got her team together and they brainstormed options for dealing with her new temperament. One solution was alprazalam, or Xanax, an anti-anxiety medication. Michelle charted Sora's response to the new medicine, in order to maintain a balance between dosage and activity level. Too much Xanax and she would just sleep; too little, and she would work herself into a frenzy. And for her, this was not a fast-acting drug—it took 40 to 60 minutes to take effect.

At this point, Michelle had already created Sora's Goo (see Chapter 5 for recipe) and was also using TTouch. She recalls, "I was in a frenzy, too, and this affected her." Michelle's mom, Carol, a human hospice nurse, suggested other medicines that are commonly used in human hospice cases. They asked the veterinarian about Ativan (lorazapam), which is a fast acting sedative. The veterinarian had no previous experience with using it in dogs, but agreed to try it. Eventually, they transitioned from the Xanax, finding that they got good results if they increased the prednisone and used Ativan as well. In spite of the fact that it was winter, Sora most enjoyed lying outside under blankets, as the cold air helped cool her body temperature and improved her breathing.

Shortly before Christmas, Michelle enlisted the help of an energy healer. After working with Sora and specifically looking into her eyes, she told Michelle that her dog's energy wasn't in her body and that she should consider getting her off so many drugs in order to get her back. Michelle feared that Sora would go into a coma, or have such a strong seizure that it would cause death, if she stopped administering the drugs. The healer helped Michelle realize that Sora's existence was in some ways artificial and that her quality of life was diminished. Michelle started weaning Sora off prednisone, but still gave her Ativan to keep her happy. At this point, her mom suggested morphine, which is also useful as an aid in respiration. The Western veterinarian she was working with was not comfortable prescribing morphine, but did offer Buprenex (buprenorphine), which turns out to be quite effective, but also very expensive. The holistic veterinarian was able to get morphine, which worked well for Sora, and made her alert, happy and improved her breathing. It worked well for five days and they were able to spend one last Christmas together.

At that point, she was running out of morphine, and due to a mishap with the prescription refill, was not able to fill the prescription. She did manage to get a little from a house call veterinarian, but felt that she had to use it sparingly so that she did not run out and leave Sora in a lot of suffering. As she dropped down the morphine dosage, it was not a smooth experience for Sora. Late on a Thursday night, shortly before she passed, she was not breathing well. She started to seize, and Michelle did not know if this was part of the natural dying process or not. The seizing gave way to irregular breathing, and Michelle called Dr. Ella Bittel from *Spirits in Transition* who was very supportive and provided her with guidance. She gave her tips on repositioning Sora, which made her more comfortable. She also spoke to the Western veterinarian clinic, and after a 45 minute phone consultation, they had a plan—with only two morphine pills left, they prescribed Buprenex and Valium, and gave the morphine rectally. Within five minutes, Sora was breathing well again. She was able to stretch out and relax until Michelle's mom arrived. And then, once the whole family was together, Sora died on January 14, 2011 at the age of ten.

Michelle and her husband moved Sora's body outside, where it was cold, and discovered she was bleeding from her mouth post-mortem. Michelle made sure that her young daughter did not see this. Sora was cremated the next day. Michelle took some of the cremains and placed them in a tin for sprinkling with some clear glitter for the benefit of her daughter. Diane Dyer of Farewells by Diane in Seattle, Washington, a local funeral celebrant who specializes in animals, performed a beautiful ceremony to commemorate Sora's life. They sprinkled ashes in a lake in early March, when the sun came out just long enough so that you could see the shimmer of the glitter on the lake, which was a beautiful scene. They also sprinkled flowers in the lake, and then went home and had tea, spending the rest of the afternoon reminiscing about Sora's life. Michelle feels that she learned so much from this experience with Sora, primarily that, as caregivers for our animals, we need to be prepared with a plan for how to address their end of life needs.

Lewis and Patty

Lewis was brought home at six weeks old from the local humane society to live with Patty and her family. Based on the date he came home and his age, they extrapolated back and chose his actual birthday as October 31, 1997, in honor of Halloween since he is primarily black. Lewis is a mixed breed, part black Lab and part Border Collie. He was always a very healthy dog, and did not experience any medical issues until he was about six years old. At that time, he required some knee surgery for meniscus problems. It was in the spring of 2009, during a routine annual visit, that his veterinarian noticed that Lewis was a bit sensitive when the rectal thermometer was inserted. During the physical exam, he felt a lump and recommended that a biopsy be taken. The diagnosis was that it was a cancer called anal sac adenocarcinoma. The veterinary surgeon felt that the tumor could be removed safely and completely, as it was small in size and concentrated in one area.

Lewis had surgery to remove the tumor on June 2, 2009. Patty also consulted a veterinary oncologist, who recommended a course of chemotherapy treatment after surgery to prevent the cancer from returning. The chemotherapy protocol called for six treatments, once every three weeks. Lewis handled the chemotherapy beautifully, and never became ill or fully lost his appetite. There were a few instances when he did not finish an entire meal in one sitting, but did ultimately finish the meal. He also did not lose any of his fur, which to this day is soft and beautiful. The week following each chemotherapy appointment, he had an appointment with their primary veterinarian, who would perform blood and temperature checks and then fax this information to the oncologist for her review. (The location of the oncologist's office was quite far from where Patty lives and so it made sense to have these tests performed locally and then easily faxed to the oncologist.)

Once the chemotherapy treatments were completed, Lewis went to his primary veterinarian once a month for a rectal examination and, every third month, he had an appointment with the veterinary oncologist. Shortly after the surgery, one of the discs in his vertebrae gave out and he required a ventral slot surgery to correct the problem. Post-surgery he developed aspiration pneumonia, which cleared up easily but was an unexpected complication.

During one of Lewis's routine veterinary appointments, another small tumor was found. Again, because the tumor was small and contained, surgery was the recommended course of treatment, again followed by a course of chemotherapy. The surgery was performed on April 28, 2011. Following the surgery, the same protocol of six chemotherapy treatments, once every three weeks, was begun. Again, Lewis has a follow up appointment with his local veterinarian once each month, and with the oncologist every third month. During the oncologist visit, an abdominal ultrasound is performed. Because this was the second occurrence of the anal sac adenocarcinoma, larger margins were removed during the second surgical procedure. Patty was warned that this could cause rectal incontinence, but she was willing to take the risk. Thankfully, Lewis has not had any issues related to the surgery.

Lewis's last chemotherapy treatment was on September 1, 2011. His laboratory results show that his kidney function is slightly off right now, but this is somewhat normal for a dog at 14 years of age. His local veterinarian now monitors his kidney functions by routinely collecting a urine sample. Throughout his battles with cancer, Patty has not changed his diet or modified supplements. Medications that Lewis has been taking for years include half of a thyroid pill; Tramadol for arthritis; Gabapentin for arthritis; and Dasuquin for joint and bone health.

Lewis's exposure to possible carcinogens has been limited, as the family does not use fertilizers in their landscaping and cannot think of any other contributing environmental factors. Patty has always fed her dogs a high quality kibble, which she supplements with white rice and chicken noodle soup.

After surviving cancer twice, Lewis is the family's miracle dog, and they remain grateful for every day that they spend with their beloved dog.

Putter and Carol

In early 2001, Putter, a Bernese Mountain Dog, came home to Carol as a puppy from a local breeder in Washington. Putter suffered from some allergies, but she seemed to be a generally healthy pup although a lot less active than other puppies Carol had raised. When she was about a year and a half, she developed "cherry eye," which occurs when one of the glands in the eye becomes prolapsed and visible. Her eye was very red, but it did not seem to bother her. Carol took her to an eye specialist and Putter had surgery to fix the problem. About a year later, Carol noticed Putter walking strangely, as if she were a Clydesdale horse walking with her legs very high, and pawing at the air in front of her. It was when Putter walked into the screen door that she realized that she was acting as if she couldn't see.

She contacted the veterinarian and brought Putter in first thing in the morning. The veterinarian confirmed that she was blind, and told Carol that it could be cancer. She was biopsied and Carol saw a specialist that afternoon with Putter. The results did indeed show stage 3 cancer, canine Hodgkins disease, a form of lymphoma. The veterinary specialist offered two options: she could either start chemotherapy, which had a 20 percent chance of success, or do nothing. He told Carol that with chemotherapy it was possible that

Putter's vision would come back, which it did shortly after the treatments began. Putter underwent chemotherapy for about a year. There was another time during treatment when she lost her vision, but the chemotherapy dosage was increased and her vision returned again. Overall, Putter tolerated the chemotherapy very well, never losing her appetite. Carol found pill pockets to be really helpful in getting Putter to take medicine.

Carol recalled that Putter would always act like a puppy with lots of energy the first few days after a chemotherapy treatment. As the weeks progressed, however, she would slow down and sleep a lot. Her glands would become very swollen. When Putter became lethargic towards the end of her life, her veterinarian offered another chemotherapy protocol as an option, but this treatment had only a 2 to 3 percent chance of success. Carol chose euthanasia at the time and stayed with Putter throughout the process. Putter went very peacefully, and closed her eyes and seemed to drift right into sleep. Carol stayed with her for a long time, and was touched by the kindness shown to her by the veterinarian and staff.

Putter was cremated and her ashes are kept in an urn. Carol kept a baby book for Putter, as well as a CD filled with photos. When she looks back on Putter's life, it is obvious to Carol that she was not a very healthy dog. By one year of age, her folder at the veterinarian was already thick. After Putter died, Carol found out that of the seven puppies in Putter's litter, at least four had cancer. She knows now that Berners are predisposed to cancer, and that European Berners have a longer lifespan (7 to 9 years) than American Berners (5 to 7 years.)

In hindsight, Carol is not sure she would have taken the same path again. She questions all of the drugs that were pumped into Putter's body during that year and wonders if it would have been easier on Putter to not proceed with the chemotherapy.

Alexander, Dave and Katie

Alexander ("Aleksei") is a purebred Samoyed who was born in Elkhart Lake, Wisconsin on April 12, 2002. When Dave and Katie Matison welcomed him into their Seattle home, he was a fluffy little bundle of joy with a mild case of idiopathic irritable bowel syndrome (IBS) which quickly cleared up. It wasn't until early April 2009 that Aleksei showed any sign that something was wrong. Dave and Katie have a high bed, and when Aleksei would jump on it, they sometimes gave him a little boost to assist. It was once when Katie helped boost Alex onto the bed that he gave a sharp yelp of pain. A few days later, he started to limp in his right rear leg. The couple took Aleksei in to see their veterinarian, but because she was on vacation, they saw a substitute veterinarian instead. After a physical examination and recap of Aleksei's medical history, the veterinarian prescribed Rimadyl (an NSAID) and advised that if the limp continued, they should bring him back in.

The limp did go away for about a week, but it returned as the dosage of Rimadyl was tapered off. They bought Aleksei back in to see their regular veterinarian this time and an X-ray was taken. While they waited for the results, Aleksei continued the Rimadyl. After a few days, the veterinarian called and told them that the radiologist's opinion was that Alex had osteosarcoma, or cancer of the bone. They immediately scheduled an appointment with the veterinary specialist, who performed a biopsy. The results revealed that Aleksei had stage 2B lymphoma, an early stage for diagnosis. At this time, the couple was advised to amputate the leg, as this was the best option for treatment of this very aggressive and painful cancer, followed by a round of chemotherapy. Their veterinarian provided them with literature about this type of cancer and they also discussed the statistics around survival

rates with and without treatment. They were told that if they chose not to treat the cancer, Aleksei could be dead within 60 days, and more likely, he would have to be euthanized after only 30 days, because of the excruciating pain caused by this type of cancer. Even with treatment, they were told that most dogs only survived between one and two years, and that in addition to the surgery, a course of chemotherapy was advisable since the cancer was likely already in Aleksei's bloodstream as well.

Faced with a very difficult decision, the couple relied on family and friends to advise and console them. Luckily, Katie's father was a doctor and he gave them the sage advice to "face the cancer head on." They took his advice and on April 24, 2009, Aleksei had his right rear leg amputated. The surgeon's report revealed that the margins were extremely clean on the tumor and that there was no evidence of metastasis. The cancer was found at the knee level, with nothing found above that point.

Three weeks after the operation, Aleksei started his chemotherapy, which was a six-month, two-drug (Carboplatin and Doxorubicin) alternating course of treatment. He did extremely well during the treatments. Side effects include slight nausea at times, slightly thinned coat and loss of his whiskers. He never lost his appetite during the treatments. His coat filled out again and his whiskers grew back once the treatment was completed. In fact, his hair is so thick that most people don't even notice that he is missing a back leg! At the time of the publishing of this book, it is three years since Aleksei has been cancer free.

To Dave and Katie, Aleksei is their miracle dog, who has truly beaten the odds and surpassed all expectations. Everywhere they go, Aleksei is always approached by people who want to pet him and take his picture. In October, 2010, Aleksei was the grand marshal of the 2 Million Dogs walk for canine cancer in King County. He and his pet cockatiel were featured in the 365 Day Dog Calendar published by Workmen's Publishers on December 8, 2011. They are continually inspired by what he has gone through and how easily he has adapted to his new physique. Thinking back on their experience, they recall that the amputation experience was horrific, and hard to deal with afterwards. At times, they questioned their decision, but when they saw how well Aleksei had adapted after only three weeks, they knew they had made the right decision. When they first brought him home, they were told to expect that it might be easier initially for Aleksei to maintain his balance on three legs while running, but not walking. After about three to four days, he figured out how to adjust his balance so that he could walk again. The couple estimates that Aleksei has about 80 percent of his previous abilities, one major difference being his ability to run; his tendency now is to trot instead. He also requires more support going up stairs.

During this process, Aleksei was not given any additional supplements. Thankfully, the Matisons had health insurance for Aleksei. The cancer limit, however, was only $3,000; the total bill was almost $14,000 for the first two years. As a follow-up, Aleksei gets a physical every month and, every third month, the visit includes an ultrasound of his soft tissue organs and X-rays of his lungs, to ensure that the cancer has not returned. According to their veterinary oncologist, lymphomas tend to re-manifest in the lungs, because of the massive amount of blood flow through the lungs. Any vaccinations are discussed carefully among the veterinarian and veterinary oncologist, as they do not want to challenge Aleksei's immune system. Decisions are based on the degree of risk to Aleksei.

Now that Aleksei is a senior dog, he takes the following supplements: chondroitin for arthritis; fish oil for heart and coat; and Tramadol as palliative treatment for the aggravation caused to his spine because he has only three legs. He also takes a mild dose of aspirin daily to address a blood clot that formed in an artery near the surgery site. It has slowly been dissolving over time.

As far as the couple knows, there is nothing in Aleksei's upbringing that seems a likely contributor to the cancer outcome. He was always fed high-quality food from their veterinarian's office, with fresh meat. Since he has always been an indoor dog, he did not get exposed to any lawn products. Dave notes that in humans, genetics are suspected as a causal factor in lymphoma cases. He has also learned of research that indicates that rapid bone growth can be a contributor as well. Irrespective of how and why Aleksei contracted lymphoma, the couple remains grateful each day that their beloved pup has beaten the odds and is still able to romp and play and bring joy to the people in his life.

Porter and Me

I decided to write this book on what to do when your best friend has cancer because my best friend, Porter, had cancer. He had hemangiosarcoma, and there were at least five tumors in his abdominal cavity by the time I knew anything was awry. I knew nothing at the time about cancer—in dogs or people—but wished I did. I had no idea what to expect in terms of personality and expected behavioral changes, how I should modify his diet or exercise, and what I could do to make him feel better. I was tortured by the fact that he could be in pain and I wouldn't know it; like many dogs, and Labs in particular, Porter was stoic when it came to pain. I learned so much along the way, so much by trial and error, that I just wished I could have had a guide as I was going through this to help me figure things out a little more quickly, so that I could have made Porter's last months a little more comfortable.

When you find out that your best friend has cancer, you are devastated. You want to devote all of your time to petting or holding your best friend, not searching the internet or scouring the library for books on cancer. I was lucky that I had people around me who gave me advice, and who did research for me so that I could devote all of my free time to taking care of Porter. My mom took out books from the library, read them and noted specific passages or chapters that I should read. She taught herself how to give Porter massages and then taught me how to do the same. Friends told me about herbs and supplements that were helpful for cancer. Other friends just let me be when I told them I couldn't talk to or see them for a while, until I'd gotten things under control. And it took a while before I'd gotten a routine together, where meal time did not take me an hour from start to finish and where I was not totally stressed out because Porter hardly ate anything I gave him.

I never expected that I would ever hear the word "cancer" from Porter's veterinarian. He'd already endured a long (and successful) battle against epilepsy, and if anything, I was concerned about a relapse of seizures, not a new disease, and certainly not cancer. One cold, rainy Seattle Sunday, I was out taking Porter and Scooby for a walk when I noticed that Porter's urine looked a little strange. At first, I convinced myself that the lack of early morning light was making me see things. But as the walk went on, I realized that something was not quite right. The telltale red tinge made me think there was blood in his urine. I couldn't stop the tears; that seemed really bad. It's bad in humans; it can't be good in dogs, either. Thankfully, our veterinarian was open on Sundays and I was able to schedule an appointment for a few hours later.

After blood work and X-rays, the doctor sent Porter's blood, urine and stool samples to the lab for testing. She also prescribed some antibiotics, saying that her best guess was that it was a kidney or urinary tract infection (UTI). She said she would call the next day when the results of all the tests were in to let me know. But by Monday midday, the red tinge was visibly absent during our walk, and I was encouraged. "Silly me," I thought, embarrassed that I had overreacted. "It's just a UTI, after all, and just see how quickly the antibiotics are working." I was not worried when I saw the familiar number of the veterinarian on my phone. It rang just as I was walking up the steps to pick up my son after school.

"I got the test results and Lola, I am so sorry. It looks like cancer," the doctor said. Cancer. Cancer. Cancer? The word seemed to be significant, but my brain wasn't really registering what the word meant. A grave feeling came over me and I paused mid-step. "What?" I asked. "It's cancer," she said. "There are multiple masses in his abdomen, and based on the blood work, it indicates cancer," she replied. I started crying. I walked back down the stairs. I didn't know what to say. She continued. "I recommend that you schedule Porter for an ultrasound, as this will help us understand what kind of cancer it is and what the treatment is." And she proceeded to give me the name of two clinics in the area that performed ultrasounds on dogs. I chose the clinic that had an oncologist on site. I figured that would be helpful.

The appointment was a few days later. I hadn't been able to talk to anyone about what was happening; I avoided all my friends and family to the extent possible. The slightest thought of cancer in Porter's body was more than I could bear and would reduce me to tears instantly. With work and taking care of my son, that was just not a viable plan. So, I isolated myself and waited for the results of the ultrasound, after which I would know more and would have a course of action to speak of.

In the meantime, I read about types of cancers in dogs on the web. I put together a list of questions to ask the veterinarian, in preparation for the ultrasound procedure.

I met with this new veterinarian that morning and asked questions about the procedure. He explained that they might want to perform a fine needle aspirate and/or biopsy and explained both procedures. Depending on where the tumors were, the fine needle aspirate might not be an option—they didn't want to puncture the tumor and risk hemorrhage. He said they would call to let me know what could be done after the ultrasound. So, I dropped Porter off and waited for a call. The doctor called just before noon, and said that, of the five tumors, they could take fine needle aspirates of only three, and did I want to proceed? Yes, I said. Again, they said they would call to let me know when he was ready to go home.

I had just gone into a team meeting when the phone rang. I rushed out of the meeting room, recognizing the number of the veterinarian clinic and not wanting to miss the call. I found a vacant office nearby, ducked in and closed the door. The veterinarian explained that it was cancer, and of the three types we had discussed as possibilities from the morning, it was the worst one—hemangiosarcoma. He explained that the best way to treat this type of cancer was with surgery. Removal of the tumor—plus a margin around the area of the tumor—was a highly effective treatment. Unfortunately, in our case, not all of the five tumors might be safely removed. One was in or on the pancreas, and just as in humans, it is not possible for dogs to live without the pancreas. One tumor was on the kidney, and while it was possible to remove a kidney, they would first need to run a few tests to ascertain whether his other kidney was functioning at full steam so as to support his system effectively. Another tumor was in his spleen, and they could easily remove it, along with two others that were in the abdominal cavity.

All these tests, all this surgery; what quality of life would Porter have throughout these procedures and ultimately, would it prove beneficial in extending his life? The fact that so many tumors were present was a sign of metastasis. Given the aggressive nature of the hemangiosarcoma cancer, it was unlikely that the cancer could be totally eradicated or reversed. In the end, I decided that all of these tests and surgeries were just too much. Porter was almost ten years old, and all I could think about was the miserable recovery period after he'd had a spleen, possibly a kidney and a large tumor removed from his abdominal cavity. Talk about stress on a system! What kind of quality of life would he have during the recovery period? We wouldn't be able to go on walks, he would be confined to the house, and he would be forced to wear a cone until the stitches were removed—at least ten to fourteen days later. It might have been different if the surgery would have removed all the cancer. If there had only been one isolated tumor in an unnecessary organ, I am sure I would have opted for surgery. Everything I had read indicated that chemotherapy was not a long-term option to prolong life in dogs, and that while side effects were not as severe as in humans, they were still unpleasant enough to affect a dog's quality of life.

I opted instead for palliative care and a more holistic path, involving homeopathy, Chinese medicine, acupuncture and lots of love and positive thinking. I wanted to just focus on him and love him and take care of him as best I could, for as long as I had. Of course, I hoped that would mean years ahead of us, but I was willing to take what I could get.

The road that lay ahead was paved with good days and bad days. There were days that we would return from the dog park and he'd be limping afterwards. This was always hard to see, so I vowed to improve the next time. I realized that a wet dog was much more likely to limp than a dry dog, so I made it a point to dry him really well with a towel whenever we went swimming. I also noticed that when wet, he was really susceptible to colder temperatures (this shouldn't have been a surprise). For that reason also, I would dry him off with a towel anytime he went swimming. Then I would wrap him in blankets while he lay down on his dog bed, and I would curl up next to him and let my body heat help to warm him back up again.

There were days that we would barely make it to the end of the block and he was ready to come home. Sometimes we'd only make it the half-block to the mailboxes, and sometimes we'd make it only to the next-door neighbors. He was always so excited to get outside and head for a walk, but some days it was just too much. He'd just lie down on the neighbor's lawn, and it might take me upwards of 15 minutes to coax him back to the house. I worried that he would get too cold lying on the grass in the winter, so I always tried to convince him as quickly as possible. Sometimes I would get overly worried that I'd never get him back in the house. But we always managed to go back inside.

There were some nights that Porter did not make the trek upstairs to my bedroom. On those nights, we slept downstairs on the couch, or occasionally, on the floor, if Porter could not make it onto the couch. Such varied sleeping accommodations worked for me because I can sleep anywhere, anytime, with any light, on almost any surface, with any distractions. (I'm also a very light sleeper since having a child and would wake very easily when I heard anyone stir in the night.)

In addition, I tried to offer as many opportunities to swim as possible, because I knew he loved it so much, and I wanted him to enjoy life to the fullest. There were times that we inadvertently overdid it, but, at the end of the day, it's a personal choice; you are the only one who knows your dog and what is right for your situation. Oh, did we have fun! Looking back, those memories are the ones that I treasure the most.

On our last night, I came downstairs after putting my son to bed to find that Porter had thrown up. This was not altogether an uncommon occurrence, so I was not overly concerned. It also turned out to be a night that he did not want to sleep upstairs. So, we slept on the couch.

Not quite two months after I'd heard the word "cancer" uttered to me on the phone by the veterinarian, Porter was in my arms dying. I had treasured every moment that I had with him, and this was no exception. I was grateful for the fact that I was there for him as he passed. My biggest worry had been that it would happen when he was alone.

So what do you need to look for? At the time, I didn't make the connection, but less than a week earlier, Porter had gone in for an acupuncture treatment, but had not perked up afterwards as had been typical. He also seemed to be a bit slower than normal. That night, he had stayed downstairs while I put my son to bed. When I came back downstairs, I saw that he had thrown up on the carpet. He also had not moved from the time I had first gone upstairs with my son. I knew this was a night I would sleep downstairs on the couch.

Porter was panting a bit more than normal when we went to bed. I remember being very tired that night, but woke up shortly thereafter to the sound of very heavy panting. I have an L-shaped sectional couch, and I was on one part of the L while he was on the other. I turned on the light and looked at him and realized that he was not doing very well.

His gums, lips and tongue were very white. I wasn't sure if he was in pain or not, but I was worried that he might be. I had had enough foresight at one of our frequent veterinarian appointments to inquire about a painkiller that I could use if I were faced with a situation where it was off-hours and I found that Porter was in pain. This was the situation I currently faced. The veterinarian had given me a few pain pills to use in this case, along with instructions on how to administer them. I followed the instructions, giving him the pill and also giving him several eyedroppers of water to help it go down.

It was early in the morning at this point, maybe 1:00 or so. There was nothing I could do but hold him, stroke him and tell him how much I loved him. My son slept soundly upstairs, Scooby lay on the dog bed, and Porter and I participated in his passing. There were many times that his breathing was so infrequent that I thought the moment had come. But each time, another low, long breath would ensue and I knew that I was spared for at least a few seconds more. I told Porter how much I loved him and that he should go whenever he was ready, that I wanted him to go when he was ready and that I didn't want him to be in any pain.

At 3:00 am, he let out a long howl, lifting his nose straight into the air all the while. When he was done, he laid his head down on my hands and then breathed his last breath. He died in my arms, just the two of us, at home, in peace. I held him for a long time after that, feeling the warmth of his fur and taking in his essence, tears everywhere. My baby, my first child, was gone. Slipped away from my very arms, right in front of me and there was not a thing I could do to stop it. I texted a friend to request help in the morning to take Porter to the veterinarian. For what exactly, I wasn't sure. I just did not know what else I should do. I sent my family and friends an email to let them know what had just happened. I sent an email to my office to let them know that I would not be in the office that day. I set the alarm for 8:00 am. I took Porter's hand in mine and then I went back to sleep. At 3:30 am, I did not know what else to do.

In the morning, Porter was stiff and cold, and the harsh reality of what had happened made me cry more. I guess this was the manifestation of that word, rigor mortis. Until that point, it had only been a word mentioned on TV police shows and movies. Now it was a word with physical meaning and emotion associated with it. My son came downstairs, and I told him the news, and we cried together for our beautiful, wonderful dog. I called my son's school and told them he would not be in that day. My friend arrived and we carried Porter into my car. It was at that point that I realized that he had excreted bodily fluids on my couch.

> *What I wish I knew at the beginning of this process is that conditions of death not only include rigor mortis, but also release of bodily fluids. Believe me, at that moment I did not care about my couch. I cleaned it later that day, washing both cover and cushions. I was on autopilot. I just did things that needed to be done, while on the inside, I was numb. I think the smell of Porter still remains, even now, as Scooby won't sit on that part of the couch for longer than a few seconds. But to us humans, there is no discernible scent or discoloration or anything. I only note this because it was a surprise to me. If you have rugs or pieces of furniture that are special, you might want to put these items in storage during the course of the treatment.*

I opted to have Porter cremated and his remains were placed in an urn that I picked up a week afterwards. When we transported Porter to the veterinarian, I had used a blanket to cover him. I am not sure why, because it is not like he was cold, but it seemed appropriate. The blanket had his smell and random fluids on it. The veterinary assistant asked if I wanted to take it with me, and I declined, because I wanted Porter to have it around him as long as possible. They asked me if I wanted it to be washed afterwards, and I told them that I didn't. Unfortunately, they did not abide by my wishes and when I picked up Porter's urn, the blanket had already been washed.

It took me months to confront their office with my disappointment and pain with what had happened. But I finally did, and while it did not bring Porter's smell back to the blanket, I felt that I stood up for his memory and honored him in one last, small way.

Jack and David

David adopted Jack from the Humane Society when he was about six months old. Jack was a mix of Labrador Retriever and possibly German Shepherd and/or other breeds. While he was always a very healthy dog, he had some funny habits that he developed pretty early on. When he was only about two to three years old, he would go outside to do his business and then he began to eat grass—about six to seven strands of the thicker wheat grass variety—after which, he would come inside and then promptly throw up. The throw up was a very yellow, bile-like mess. After throwing up, Jack would eat his breakfast, but would keep that down. Even though Jack was a Lab, David recalls instances where he would put food down, but Jack wouldn't eat it until the early evening, and then would still eat his dinner a few hours after that. After this continued, David took Jack to the veterinarian, but was told that "well, some dogs just do that."

Later on however, Jack started to throw up in the house while David was away at work. This would occur in spurts, where he would

throw up for three days in a row, but would be okay for five days in a row. Occasionally, he would throw up immediately after eating, but more typically, it happened in the middle of the night. After about a month of this behavior, David took Jack back to the veterinarian, who thought it could be a reaction to the food. So she prescribed a different diet and recommended more soft food versus kibble. He tried this, but it didn't make any difference. The veterinarian then suggested that they try to isolate what he was eating.

David started to do his own research about dog nutrition. Up until that point, he had always purchased dog food from the grocery store, but he quickly learned through his research that this was not a high-quality form of dog food. So he went to the local pet store instead, and started to purchase a higher-quality food. While the switch to better food helped Jack's appetite, it did not affect the vomiting. Next, the veterinarian recommended a bland diet. This helped for a few weeks, but then the throwing up resumed.

For about three to four months they tried many different diets and varied food strategies. For example, the veterinarian thought Jack might just have a very acidic stomach, and so recommended that David leave food out at night. But nothing seemed to make a difference. At this point, the next step was to get an ultrasound of his stomach and possibly a biopsy. The ultrasound revealed that there was a thickening of the stomach wall, but nothing more conclusive than that. In March of 2011, a biopsy was performed and that is when David received the diagnosis of lymphoma of the stomach. It was T-cell lymphoma, which is more aggressive than B-cell lymphoma.

David took Jack to see a veterinary oncologist, who explained a variety of chemotherapy protocols that could be used to treat Jack, and recommended the Madison Wisconsin protocol. She provided David with sobering statistics of average survival time without treatment, only two months, and with treatment, about six to eight months. She noted that in Jack's case, because it was located in a digestive organ, his body was weakened because he was not able to eat and keep up his strength. First, she suggested that they get a second opinion and asked her specialist to perform another ultrasound check, since she was interested in confirming the stage of the cancer. The second ultrasound confirmed the thickening of the stomach wall, and based on the ultrasound alone, did not confirm it was cancer, since there was no presence of a tumor and the lymph nodes were not enlarged. They reached the conclusion that the cancer was likely caught at an early stage.

Chemotherapy was started immediately at the first visit around mid-March. The Madison Wisconsin protocol lasts a full six months, with weekly treatments the first two months and treatments every other week for the remaining four months. At this point, David started to keep a diary, where he noted that Jack was already in remission by mid-April. Frequent ultrasounds were performed throughout the six months to monitor the condition of Jack's stomach and to ensure that the cancer did not return. Once Jack completed the full protocol, they began monthly visits to the veterinarian for blood work and vitals and visits to the oncologist every two months for an ultrasound.

Jack was now back to his normal self and David was feeding him a very high-quality, grain-free dog food. Interestingly enough, Jack did not go back to his habitual grass eating behavior as before. He did it only occasionally, and was more finicky about the type of grass he would eat. Around December 2011, he started to throw up again, but only intermittently. David was wary, and continued to monitor Jack's behavior, noting all of the changes in his diary. When he saw the same pattern from the previous year, he informed the oncologist at their next visit. Unfortunately, the cancer had come back. Jack is now undergoing his second round of chemotherapy, again the Madison Wisconsin protocol. David has noted that this second round of treatment is hitting harder this time. After returning home from a treatment, David recalls that Jack just lay down and hardly moved for two days. During this time, he was completely knocked out and wouldn't eat or drink. David has also noticed that the side effects of each chemotherapy treatment last longer, such as diarrhea, night restlessness and gas.

He will be done with this second round of treatment in September of 2012. As before, he has gone into remission already and the growth in his stomach wall has retreated. He has stopped throwing up and his appetite is back again. David hopes that this second treatment will allow him to enjoy Jack's company for many years to come. You can do it, Jack!

Jasper and Me

I became a volunteer at *Pasado's Safe Haven* animal sanctuary in mid-November 2009 and my first responsibility was to walk dogs—a dream job for me! After two weeks, I knew the dogs by name and there was one dog in particular, named Bob, who stood out for me. He was a barker, but as I approached his enclosure, he'd stop barking. He was great on the leash on our walks and appeared to be a yellow Lab mix of some sort. He seemed very sad to me, and would never look me in the eye, even when I knelt down beside him to scratch his ears and talk to him. On the spur of the moment, I decided to adopt him and brought him home on the evening of November 28, 2009. The next day, we went to a local do-it-yourself dog wash and gave him a bath. We also gave him a new name: Jasper.

I scheduled an appointment with my veterinarian for the following week to look him over and establish a baseline. He was very skinny so I wanted to learn more about how to put some weight on him safely. The sanctuary had rescued him from the Seattle Humane Society, and little was known about his medical history, other than that he had been picked up at an intersection in Federal Way, Washington. While his papers indicated he was around seven years of age, I suspected he was closer to ten; my veterinarian concurred with my assessment.

Jasper quickly became a beloved member of our family, and assimilated well into our daily routine. On September 14, 2010, Jasper started throwing up every meal and drooling more than normal. He was still drinking water during this time, but there were no other symptoms. I stopped feeding him his normal food and switched to rice and chicken broth, but he could not keep any food down. This went on for a couple of days, and so I scheduled an appointment for him. The veterinarian performed an examination and determined that Jasper was nauseous, but did not know why. Blood work was taken and I was referred to another clinic that could perform an X-ray, so that we could evaluate what might be happening internally. There was a suspicion that perhaps Jasper had swallowed a foreign object that was now lodged somewhere in his digestive system.

While we waited for the test results, the veterinarian prescribed Cerenia for the nausea, and suggested that I make meals of white rice and cooked chicken, with a small amount of canned pumpkin, as well as powdered colostrum, to strengthen his immune system. This seemed to work. Once on the Cerenia, Jasper ate well through the weekend, and I felt like we had turned a corner and were on the road to recovery. The X ray results did now show a blockage, so we were still unsure as to the root cause. On Monday, September 20, 2010, Jasper refused to eat. This was a bad sign. Jasper was the most food motivated dog I have ever known, and for him to refuse food was unheard of. I went to work that day not knowing what to do next. About an hour later, I called the veterinary specialist clinic and made an appointment for an ultrasound in the next hour.

Prior to the ultrasound, the specialist, a veterinary internist, told me that if they saw anything suspicious in the ultrasound, they would immediately do a fine needle aspirate. They were not sure how long the procedure would take, as it was based on what they saw and if aspirates were necessary. When the internist returned a while later, the news was not good. The ultrasound revealed that he had multiple lesions on his liver and spleen; the cytology of the liver indicated that it was cancer, mast cell tumors. Even worse was the fact that it was in the late stages and had already metastasized.

Two days later, we met with a veterinary oncologist, who gave a poor prognosis for Jasper. She felt that, due to the aggressive nature of the cancer, he would have one to two months to live with no treatment and perhaps three to five months if chemotherapy were pursued. At a minimum, she suggested that I continue with the Cerenia, but also purchase some over-the-counter human medicines, Pepcid AC as a stomach protectant and Benadryl as an anti-histamine and mast cell stabilizer. In addition, she prescribed prednisone, which has a mild anti-cancer effect and would help to stabilize the mast cell tumors, decrease the risk of a degranulation event and would generally make Jasper feel better.

> In the case of my dog with mast cell tumor, at best chemotherapy might have given us an extra four months. While an additional four months with him would have been wonderful, I had to think about what the quality of our life

> *would be like during those four months: the weekly visits to the veterinary oncologist and our regular veterinarian for shots and monitoring; the side effects due to the chemotherapy treatments, including vomiting, diarrhea, lethargy, and decreased appetite; and the imminence of the ultimate outcome looming over us. Was it worth it to put him through these treatments, just so that I could have more time with him? I decided, ultimately, to proceed with hospice care, so that we could focus on enjoying each new day together. Also, while most dogs tend to handle chemotherapy treatments with only the mild side effects listed above, some may become very ill and have profuse vomiting, dehydration, diarrhea, and/or suffer a decrease in white blood cell count, increasing the risk of infection.*

Later that day, I took Jasper to our regular veterinarian and we discussed the recommendations made by the oncologist. Given the cancer was so advanced, I did not see the benefit of putting him through weekly chemotherapy treatments. He would have to endure the stress of these visits and any side effects of the chemotherapy. While fewer than 15 percent of pets have some side effect, most are mild such as vomiting, diarrhea, lethargy, or decreased appetite. In some cases, the effects can be life threatening and require hospitalization. We agreed that the best course of action in my case was to continue the Cerenia, and begin the Pepcid AC, Benadryl and prednisone, with Tramadol for pain, if needed.

Jasper had a reaction to the prednisone, one of the 5 percent of dogs do not tolerate this drug well. In addition to being extremely lethargic, he would not eat or drink and did not want to urinate. He could not stand or walk without support. There were a few times that day that I was convinced I was going to lose him, but frequent calls to my veterinarian for advice helped us survive the day. He stressed that we should get Jasper up and moving and that we should hydrate him. This definitely helped. Needless to say, I did not use the prednisone again.

From that point on, Jasper would have some occasional bad days, but most days, we were able to take our walks and he was able to eat his meals. I switched to the same high-quality canned dog foods that had helped get Porter through his battle with cancer. Jasper loved them! I also used a Bach flower essence, honeysuckle, to help me let Jasper and my grief go. Most nights, I slept downstairs on the couch, as Jasper no longer ventured upstairs. He would wake several times during the night to urinate, so it was easier to spend the night downstairs. There were countless times during these weeks when Jasper would lose bladder control in the house, sometimes vomiting or defecating as well.

Throughout this period, Jasper seemed so tired, and would often lie in the same spot for hours without moving. He particularly enjoyed being outside during this time. On his last day, he spent a few hours outside in the sun, on the grass, and had trouble getting back into the house. I carried him inside and realized later in the evening that his gums were white. I knew the end was close, and even though I had blankets nearby, I forgot to place them underneath his body. When he breathed his last breath, his legs stretched out and then he was gone. It was October 13, 2010, only 23 days after I received his cancer diagnosis.

We brought Jasper's body to the veterinarian to be cremated. I remembered to cut a lock of his hair. On the anniversary of his death, I go to his favorite places and spread his ashes. I treasure his memory in the pictures and videos and stories that capture the short time he was a member of our family.

Blake and Sarah

Blake is a black and tan mutt, with some Rottweiler, German Shepherd and Labrador Retriever all mixed in. He is about 11 years old now, and Sarah adopted him when he was around a year old, back in Michigan. Blake was always very healthy, minus one bout of Coonhound Paralysis, a peripheral nerve disorder that is thought to be related to exposure to raccoons, although this is not proven. Blake was paralyzed and spent a short time in the doggie ICU, where he received treatment. The condition afflicted him in September 2004 and he was walking again in December 2004.

It was not until the summer of 2008 that Sarah noticed a bump on the side of Blake's snout. At first, she didn't think much of it, but then noticed that it was painful for him, as he would cry and pull away when she touched it. She happened to meet a veterinary technician at a softball game, and she asked if she would take a look at it. The technician suggested she have it checked out. Since Blake was due for a teeth cleaning, which required sedation, Sarah asked the veterinarian to also remove the bump. Blake started a course of antibiotics after the removal of the bump. At this point, Sarah had no idea that it was cancerous.

In September 2008, another mass was removed, which was found to be cancerous, a nasal spindle-cell tumor. Because of the tumor's location, it could not be removed completely, so Sarah was referred to a veterinary oncologist. The oncologist recommended that Sarah take Blake to Washington State University for radiation therapy, a more preferred treatment for such a localized tumor. For about four weeks, Blake was boarded at the WSU School of Veterinary Medicine, where he was sedated and received a daily dose of radiation targeted at his nose. During his stay, a veterinary student was assigned to his care. Because the tumor was considered a low-high grade tumor, a more aggressive, curative protocol of 18 gray (a unit of measure of the dose of absorbed radiation) was applied to attempt to completely eradicate it. While the radiation specialist thought the tumor was low-grade, there was some concern it was a more aggressive, high-grade tumor. Since this type of cancer has a high propensity of recurrence, the curative approach was chosen.

When Blake was finally able to return home in November 2008, he looked great—at first. Sarah recalls that a week later, he suffered from radiation burns, his hair fell out, his face was swollen, and the radiation site was weepy and irritated. He lost interest in playing, and licked the area constantly. For about three weeks, he looked awful, with a crusty, swollen muzzle. Sarah was told that his hair might never grow back, or that it might grow back in an unusual way. His long spindly whiskers have not returned, but the rest of the hair on his muzzle has.

Since his treatment, Blake sees the veterinary oncologist every three months for a recheck, which involves a physical exam, including his lymph nodes. On his most recent visit, the oncologist felt that he was in remission long enough and could push the visits out to every six months. Every year, he receives a chest X-ray to check for metastasis in the lungs. About 18 months ago, Sarah noticed some unusual symptoms. Blake had a lot of nasal discharge, licked the roof of his mouth constantly, and made strange yawning sounds as though something was bothering him. Sarah took him for a cat scan (CT scan) of his head, and learned that he has nerve damage from the radiation, which has resulted in chronic rhinitis, irritation and inflammation of nasal tissues, and a little bit of neuralgia, pain in the nerves. To combat the symptoms, Blake takes an NSAID, Deramaxx, daily. He is also taking Gabapentin to control his pain.

Sarah describes Blake as "near-scented" these days, as his sense of smell is not as good as it once was, and he gets close to objects in order to smell them. He also snores terribly and makes occasional weird facial movements. Almost four years later, Blake is still cancer-free and enjoying life with his family at home. While Sarah has not calculated the full cost of all Blake's treatments, she recalls that the radiation

therapy alone was over $5,000, and the CT scan was $1,000. She often wonders if the dog park in Michigan that she used to take Blake to was the cause of his cancer, after she learned that the water around the park contained dioxane, a known carcinogen to animals. Irrespective, though, she remains thrilled each day to have Blake in her life.

Resources

Books

Brevitz, Betsey, DVM. *The Complete Healthy Dog Handbook*. Workman Publishing Company, Inc., New York, New York, 2009.

Eldredge, Debra M., DVM and Margaret H. Bonham. *Cancer and Your Pet: The Complete Guide to the Latest Research, Treatments and Options*. Capitol Books, Inc., Sterling, Virginia, 2005.

Kaplan, Laurie. *Help Your Dog Fight Cancer: An Overview of Home Care Options*. JanGen Press, Briarcliff, New York, 2005.

Martin, Ann. *Food Pets Die For*. New Sage Press, Troutdale, Oregon, 1997.

Messonnier, Shawn DVM. *8 Weeks to a Healthy Dog: An Easy-to-Follow Program for the Life of Your Dog*. Rodale, 2003.

Messonnier, Shawn DVM. *Natural Health Bible for Dogs & Cats*. Prima Publishing, Roseville, CA, 2001.

Messonnier, Shawn DVM. *The Natural Vet's Guide to Preventing and Treating Cancer in Dogs*. New World Library, Novato, California, 2006.

Morrison, Wallace B. *Cancer in Dogs & Cats: Medical & Surgical Management*. Teton New Media, Jackson, Wyoming, 2002.

Pasek, KaLee R., DVM. *Honoring the Journey: A Guided Path Through Pet Loss*. Self-published, 2008.

Pitcairn, Richard H. VM, PhD and Susan Hubble Pitcairn. *Dr. Pitcairn's Complete Guide to Natural Health for Dogs and Cats, 3rd Edition*. Rodale Press, Inc., Emmaus, Pennsylvania, 2005.

Quackenbush, Jamie and Denise Graveline. *When Your Pet Dies: How to Cope with Your Feelings*. Pocket Books, New York, 1988.

Reynolds, Rita. *Blessing the Bridge: What Animals Teach Us About Death, Dying, and Beyond*. New Sage Press, Troutdale, Oregon, 2001.

Rinpoche, Sogyal. *The Tibetan Book of Living and Dying*. Harper One, New York, 2002.

Schultze, Kymythy R. CCN, AHI. *Natural Nutrition for Dogs and Cats: The Ultimate Diet*. Hay House Inc., Carlsbad, CA, 1999.

Straw, Deborah. *Why Is Cancer Killing Our Pets? How You Can Protect and Treat Your Animal Companion*. Healing Arts Press, Rochester, Vermont, 2000.

Articles

Bergman, PJ, et al. "Development of a xenogeneic DNA vaccine program for canine malignant melanoma at the Animal Medical Center." *Vaccine* 2006; 24:4582-4585.

Epstein, Mark E., DVM, DABVP, CVPP, "CVC Highlight: Opioids: The good, the bad, and the future." *Veterinary Medicine*, December, 2011. Can be read online at: http://veterinarymedicine.dvm360.com/vetmed/Medicine/Opioids-The-good-the-bad-and-the-future/ArticleStandard/Article/detail/752238?contextCategoryId=42377.

Audios

28 Days of Grief and Healing Transforming the Loss of a Beloved Animal Companion, Claire Chew, MA, 2011.

Websites for articles, research and products

FDA News Release, FDA: *First Drug to Treat Cancer in Dogs Approved.* June, 2009. http://www.fda.gov/NewsEvents/Newsroom/PressAnnouncements/2009/ucm164118.htm.

End of Life Hospice Care: The Human-Animal Bond at the End of Life Hospice Care, The American Association of Human-Animal Bond Veterinarians, 2012. http://aahabv.org/index.php/end-of-life-hospice-care.

A Guide to Prescription NSAIDs for Canine Arthritis: Common Brand Name Canine NSAIDs. http://www.vetinfo.com/prescription-nsaid-arthritis.html.

Treating Chronic Pain in Dogs. http://www.dogaware.com/health/chronicpain.html.

Guides to cancer diagnosis and treatment. http://www. petcancercenter.org/.

Lap of Love, Veterinary Hospice and In-Home Euthanasia, www.lapoflove.com, offers a fee service for families who have just received a cancer diagnosis for their pet that provides a 30-45 minute phone or Skype consultation with a veterinary oncologist. For more information on fees and services, contact Dr. Dani McVety, at DrDani@LapofLove.com or 813-407-9441.

Georgia's Legacy, Canine Cancer Resource. http://www.fightcaninecancer.com/.

Pet Cancer Awareness and the Blue Buffalo Foundation for Cancer Research. http://www.petcancerawareness.org/.

Doctors Foster and Smith Cancer Articles. http://www.peteducation. com/category.cfm?c=2+1638.

Information and Inspiration for canine cancer, clinical trial information, diet and nutrition and Essiac tea. http://www.caninecancer. com/.

Bach Flower Essences for Pets. http://www. bachremedies.com, http://www.rescueremedy.com/pets, www.nelsonbach. com.

Basics of some cancers and treatments. http://www.labbies.com/cancerintro.htm.

Integrative Treatment of Cancer in Dogs. http://www.ehow.com/list_6805769_cancer-dogs-care-treatment-alternatives.html.

Naturally Treating Epilepsy and Seizure Disorders. http://www.purelypets. com/articles/epilepsyarticle.htm.

Long-Term Health Risks and Benefits Associated with Spay/Neuter in Dogs. http://www. naiaonline.org/pdfs/LongTermHealthEffects OfSpayNeuterInDogs.pdf.

Pet Loss and Grief Support. http://www.petloss.com/.

List of Veterinary Teaching Hospitals. http://landofpuregold.com/cancer/vet.htm.

List of clinical studies at University of Guelph. http://www.ovc. uoguelph.ca/clin/faculty/.

Holistic care and natural nutrition. http://www.kymythy. com/index.html.

Morris Animal Foundation of Colorado. http://www.curecaninecancer.org/.

Complementary and alternative veterinary medicine. http://altvetmed.org/.

Music to support canine immune and nervous systems. http://www. throughadogsear.com/.

Network of animal professionals. http://animalwellness.ning.com/.

Diagnostic testing and titering for pets and animal blood bank. http://www.hemopet.org/

Dr. Demian Dressler, "Chronic Morphine May Worsen Dog Cancer." Dog Cancer Blog. http://www.dogcancerblog.com/chronic-morphine-may-worsen-dog-cancer/.

Guidelines for Veterinary Hospice Care. http://www.avma.org/issues/policy/hospice_care.asp.

Canine Melanoma Vaccine Information. http://petcancervaccine. com/vaccine/index.shtml.

Articles on Canine Cancer Vaccines. http://landofpuregold.com/ cancer/vaccine.htm.

New England Pet Hospice. http://www.newenglandpethospice. com/.

Post memorial photos and memories. http://www.vetmed.wsu. edu/ PetMemorial/.

Children's Story about a Dog with Cancer Named Bo. http://every-onelovesbo.blogspot.com/p/bos-book-for-kids.html.

Spirits in Transition. http://spiritsintransition.org/.

Dr. Johanna Budwig's Healing Diet and Protocol. http://www.heal-ingcancernaturally.com/.

Veterinary Oncologist website. http://www.helpingpetswithcancer. com.

Dr. Jean Dodds's Canine Vaccination Protocol. http://www.itsforth-eanimals.com/DODDS-CHG-VACC-PROTOCOLS.HTM.

Blog on grief. http://griefpraylove.blogspot.com/.

Supplements for pets sold to veterinary professionals. http://www. rxvitamins. com/pet/index.php.

Mushroom supplements. http://www.mushroommatrix.com/.

Essiac tea. http://www.essiacinfo.org/.

Apocaps, a nutraceutical supplement for canine cancer. http:// apocaps.com/.

Hoxsey/Boneset supplement for intense bone pain associated with osteosarcoma. http://shop.petsage.com/WORLD-HERBS-FOR-PETS-HOXSEY_BONESET/productinfo/NM-X-07884/.

General supplements. http://shop. petsage. com/.

Seacure Protein. http://www. seacure-protein. com/.

Glossary

Acupuncture. A component of Traditional Chinese Medicine whereby fine needles are inserted into the body at certain key points. The treatment is often used to relieve pain and can also be used to release the flow of energy, or chi, in the body.

Anechoic. Lacking an echo, pertaining to an ultrasound.

Antiangiogenesis. The prevention of the development of blood vessels.

Apoptosis. A normal part of the life cycle of a cell where the cell dies. This is also called programmed cell death.

Biopsy. In most cases, a minor surgery that involves the removal of a small sample of tissue from a tumor or growth that is then analyzed to determine the cause of a disease.

Cancer Cachexia. "Cancer Cachexia is a condition that can develop secondary to cancer. A cachexic dog experiences drastic and progressive weight loss regardless of the quality or quantity of food eaten. He becomes unable to metabolize nutrients and, eventually, reaches a state of severe malnutrition. Once cachexia has developed, it is usually not reversible even if cancer treatment achieves a cure or a remission. There are varying opinions on this topic, but a low-carbohydrate, high-fat diet may decrease the likelihood of a dog with cancer developing cancer cachexia." [*Veterinary Oncology Secrets*, editor

Robert C. Rosenthal, DVM, PhD. Hanley & Belfus, Inc, 2001, p. 107]

Carcinoma. A malignant tumor that is derived from epithelial cells, those that line the inside of the body or cover an area inside the body. This type of cancer metastasizes to other parts of the body.

Caudal. Indicates that something is related to the tail or hind end of an animal.

Cavitated. Indicates the presence of cavities, where none would normally exist.

Cytology. The study of cells, particularly as it relates to their appearance and structure, used to indicate the absence of presence of medical conditions.

Degranulation event. The release of large amounts of chemicals (naturally found in the body), such as histamine, heparin, proteolytic enzymes, etc., without any warning. This is one of the more challenging aspects of dealing with mast cell tumors.

Diffuse. Spread out.

Echogenicity. The act of reflecting or generating sound waves.

Epithelial cells. Cells that line the inside of the body or cover an area inside the body.

Fibrosarcoma. A malignant tumor that most often occurs in bone tissue, but may also occur in soft tissues or organs.

Fine needle aspirate. An outpatient procedure performed in conjunction with ultrasound, whereby a long fine needle is passed into an organ or tumor to retrieve a small sample of cells that is then analyzed to determine cause of disease.

Hematuria. Indicates the presence of blood in the urine.

Hepatopathy. Indicates the presence of a diseased liver.

Holistic veterinary medicine. A type of veterinary medicine that incorporates non-Western modalities, such as homeopathy, Chinese herbs, and acupuncture.

Homeopathy. A branch of alternative medicine that employs small doses of highly diluted remedies to cure various ailments and diseases by stimulating the body to heal itself. It was developed in the late 1700's by a German physician.

Homotoxicology. Treatments that integrate homeopathy with conventional medicine. This method was developed over fifty years ago in Germany.

Hypoechoic. Indicates the presence of an increased echo.

Lipoma. A fatty tumor, typically benign, that is located under the skin. They generally affect older animals.

Lymphoma, or lymphosarcoma. A tumor, typically malignant, that is located in lymph tissue or lymph nodes.

Margins. The area around a tumor that is removed during surgery to increase the likelihood that all cancerous cells are removed.

Maxillary. Relating to the jaw or jawbone.

Metastasis. Describes the condition when a cancer confined to a certain organ or area of the body, spreads to a different part of the body, indicating that the cancer is aggressively and actively growing.

Naturopathic veterinary medicine. See Holistic veterinary medicine.

Neoplasia. Indicates new tissue growth.

Peritoneal. Related to the lining of the abdomen.

Sarcoma. A malignant tumor that usually occurs in connective tissue.

Sulforaphane. A compound that is found in cruciferous vegetables that is believed to detoxify carcinogens in the body.

Synovial. A fluid found in joints.

Traditional Chinese Medicine (TCM). Medical practices that originated in China and have been in use for over 2000 years. These include acupuncture, herbal medicine, massage, and dietary therapy.

Ultrasound (ultrasonograph). A medical imaging technique that provides insight regarding what is happening internally in the body, providing a 2-D representation of internal organs and cavities. Ultrasounds also reveal the presence or absence of blood flow, which may help better diagnose a tumor or mass.

Sample End Plan

Our beloved dog, _____, is nearing the end of his/her life. We'd like to outline how we would like to handle his/her passing, when the time comes.

1. Who should be present:
   - Family Member #1
   - Family Member #2
   - ...
   - Friend #1
   - Friend #1
   - ...

2. Environment:
   - Ideally, we would like our beloved dog, _____, to pass naturally, in his/her own time, at home.
   - We'd like soft lights.
   - We'd like no noise or interruptions. Phone ringers should be turned off.
   - We have soft towels and blankets nearby that should be placed underneath our dog when the time is close.
   - We'd like for our family and close friends to be present.
   - ....

3. Post-Mortem:

- o Afterwards, we would like to have private time with our dog to mourn and grieve.

- o We plan to keep his/her body at home for ___ hours/days.

- o We'll need to have the following items on hand:

- o Bags of ice

- o Pan or box

- o Clean towels and blankets

- o We plan to bury/cremate our dog ___ days after he/she passes.

- o Here is the name of our veterinarian: _____

- o This is how we will transport our dog, if necessary: _____

- o We'd like to take a small cutting of his/her fur for our memories, from his/her tail/coat/etc.

- o ...

- o ...

Whitepaper:
Nutrition and Canine Cancer
Causes, Prevention and Recovery

Author: Shelly Fuller, owner and Pet Nutritionist for Paws Café in Redmond, Washington

Cancer is one of the leading causes of death in dogs. Certain breeds, such as the Bernese Mountain Dog and Retrievers, are reported to be at an even greater risk of cancer with affliction rates thought to be as high as 50-70%.

The National Canine Cancer Institute, a nationwide, non-profit corporation dedicated to eliminating cancer as a major health issue, has identified 39 different types of cancer in dogs. They have created a vast library of resources to help veterinarians and pet owners understand what the symptoms are for early detection, the most common diagnostic tools used to identify the different types of cancer, drug and surgical therapies that are most commonly used in treatment and the prognosis for each type of cancer.

There are many similarities in the cancers that we find in dogs and humans, but there is a vast disparity in research and mindshare between the species when it comes to actual treatment options. For example, in the 60s and 70s, dogs were used for experimental testing of lymphoma and stem cell treatments for humans. Dogs were a better candidate for this testing than other species because they have such a complex genetic diversity, second only to humans. The main issue that scientists ran into with their early tests was tissue rejection.

By testing on dogs, it became apparent that the donor tissue needed to closely resemble the recipient in order for the transplant to be successful. Bone marrow transplants are risky and are therefore limited in their use, even in human patients with life-threatening conditions. Still, they have been a viable treatment option now for many years. In the meantime, hundreds of thousands of dogs have been diagnosed with lymphoma every year and their treatment options have been limited to chemotherapy and radiation which offer a survival rate of approximately two years, verses an estimated 50-60% cure rate with the bone marrow transplant. There have been a few "cutting-edge" veterinarians that have elected to perform the transplant procedure but it wasn't until 2004 that Dr. Edmund Sullivan of Bellingham, Washington, performed the first *official* (and successful) bone marrow treatment in this region on a dog for the purpose of curative therapy for a cost of approximately $25,000 dollars.

In much the same way that a disparity exists between human and dog cancer therapies, there is a disparity in the traditional and holistic views on the overall treatment options available today, or even those forthcoming. Traditionalists believe that treatment options involve surgery, chemotherapy, radiation and that the most promising future advances in treatment include targeted delivery of gene, protein, hormone, and enzyme therapies. Holistic minded practitioners look to nutrition, supplement, and even energy therapies as less invasive treatment options that they believe are just as effective but that can be employed early as a cancer prevention program. The challenge for them, with regards to credibility, is that they rarely have the large scale funding to back their claims with actual verifiable research. So, in much the same way as Dr. Sullivan took the first steps in canine bone marrow therapy, an increasing number of holistic practitioners are stepping forward to collate their vast amounts of professional experience in the areas of preventative and nutritional therapies to increase awareness of these options.

The rest of this white paper will focus on the holistic component of nutrition and what role it may play in the cause, prevention and recovery of dogs with cancer.

Causes

You are what you eat.

Before the wide spread availability of commercial pet foods (following World War II), dogs were fed table scraps consisting primarily of meat. Some dogs were opportunistic hunters and supplemented their diets with small rodents and mammals. At first, the goal of commercial dog food was much the same as it was for military personnel at the time; manufacturers wanted foods that wouldn't spoil quickly and were inexpensive and quick to make. That meant that they needed to be simplistic, dry foods that were high in inexpensive grain and low in meat, fresh fruits, or vegetables.

Because of this sudden change in their diet, dogs, for the first time in their evolution, started to gain extreme amounts of weight, develop allergies that caused their ears to become inflamed and their skin to itch profusely, and they developed severe dental disease because of the sugars in their high carb diets. This, however, was just the start of it.

By the mid 1950s, food scientists had made significant progress in the creation of various food ingredients that would go even further to replace real foods sources and extend shelf life beyond anything that had previously been possible. Think of this time period as the "Twinkie" era because it was the perfect example of how something as simple as a snack cake could include so few natural ingredients. Dog food manufacturers incorporated many of these new engineered ingredients into their foods and in doing so increased their profit share, as well as improved their (human) customer satisfaction. Human consumers liked the new products because it meant that they could buy large bags of food, very affordably, that could last several weeks in a closet pantry. Little did we know at the time, what the cost would really be for those conveniences in terms of their dog's long term health & well-being.

I believe, as do many others, that a fair number of the diseases we see today in both dogs and humans are the result of scientifically altered, processed foods that are high in starchy carbohydrates. Some of these ingredients have been proven to cause cancer, yet still they remain in some of the largest brands available. Science Diet, for example, a food sold & recommended by many Veterinarians, contains two known cancer causing preservatives, Ethoxyquin and BHT.

Not all Veterinarians were quick to recommend these foods however. Veterinarians that had been in practice for many years during this feeding transition witnessed the decline in health first hand, noting that there had been a shift from treating infectious diseases such as distemper to treating chronic degenerative diseases such as cancer, diabetes, liver disease, heart disease, and so forth. Those that were convinced that diet change was responsible for these diseases reached out to overseeing authorities to voice their concerns but by the time these observations were made, pet food had become a very powerful industry.

If you look at any grocery store dog food label today, not only is there a lot of cheap filler grains but now, thanks to the food scientists, there is also a long list of chemically altered meat-by-products, unidentifiable, chemically formulated binders, fillers, artificial flavors, and preservatives. Do all of these ingredients cause cancer? Probably not, but if these artificial, chemically altered foods are the only source of nutrition the animal is provided, isn't it safe to assume that the dog's health is critically challenged? It's the subtle, long term damage of these foods that is so insidious. I've seen many young dogs appear to thrive on these diets only to become obese and develop chronic allergies by the time they are two years old. Later, as these dogs approach their sixth, seventh, or eighth birthday, the degenerative diseases take over. Within a few meager years, the vast majority of these animals will have succumbed to their diseases. How many dogs die of old age anymore?

In the past two decades, there have been several outspoken opponents of the pet food industry. Dr. Pitcairn and Ann Martin are two very well known authors on the subject. Dr. Pitcairn conducted feeding trials on cats fed raw food back in the 80s that is still well circulated in support of the "feed raw" movement. What his study showed was that cat's fed raw unadulterated food lived longer, had healthier kittens, and fewer health issues. His studies went on to show that a cat's health can demise quickly once it is moved to commercial, high processed food, and that it can take as long as three generations to undo the damage of feeding such a diet. It's a pretty strong argument and a large part of the reason I switched my own cats to raw and later entered the field of pet nutrition. Ann Martin showed how corrupt the pet food industry had become with little to no regulation in place to protect our household pets. She horrified us with stories of rendered cats and dogs making their way back into our pet's food.

A handful of manufacturers listened and made changes. Some households no longer trusted the pet food industry and began feeding home prepared foods. The natural pet food segment has grown an average of 10% a year over the past 5-10 years and with more and more natural pet food manufacturers joining the movement, many pets are on their way to becoming healthy again. Sadly, with this amount of growth, the industrial commercial pet food industry is trying to carve their way into this space with false and misleading advertising. This industry has in fact, become so large now (approximately 42 billion annually) that it's practically unstoppable as long as people continue to believe them. The best hope of the holistic pet care providers is that we are able to educate as many pet families as possible to the real facts to prevent the needless pain and suffering of our greatest companion.

Prevention

Simply put, the healthiest thing that anyone can do for their dog to prevent cancer is to feed them a fresh, raw food diet consisting of quality hormone and antibiotic free meats and organic vegetables and fruits. Don't allow marketing scams to convince you that you need to add a bunch of synthetic supplements. Nature really does know better.

Many experts believe that the immune system is only as strong as the digestive tract is healthy. For that reason, I think that it is to every dog's benefit to receive a daily dose of quality probiotics, the good bacteria the keep our gut healthy, increase nutrient absorption, and stave off bad bacteria, yeast overgrowth, and unhealthy fermentation gases that can lead to bloat, the number two cause of death in dogs.

If your dog needs an anti-inflammatory for a joint condition, try natural fish oils that are high in Omega 3s. Always buy human grade oils that are tested for metals and PCBs.

If you have a breed of dog that is at a higher risk of developing cancer, supplement with herbs that are high in antioxidants such as Resveratrol, a component of grape skins. This supplement has received the seal of approval from the National Canine Cancer Foundation. Red Clover is also commonly used as a blood purifier and anti-cancer herb.

Another factor worth consideration in our understanding of cancers in dogs is the effect that spaying and neutering has on them. Historically, there has been a lot of information available on the prevention of mammary cancer in female dogs. Now, we are starting to see a broader picture of the effects that spaying and neutering has with regards to cancer in dogs specific to different age brackets. See this website for more details: (http://www. naiaonline. org/pdfs/Long-TermHealthEffectsOfSpayNeuterInDogs. pdf)

Recovery

It's never too late to start feeding your dog healthy food; even if it's simply to keep your ailing dog eating and comfortable in his final days.

For those that are fortunate enough to receive successful treatment for their cancer early, it's more important than ever to adopt a good healthy diet & lifestyle.

Dogs are social creatures. They need fresh air and walks beyond their own property lines to appreciate the value of living. The power of positive thought exists with all living, thinking beings.

The appropriate fresh food diet for a dog recovering from cancer depends on the status of their treatment. A dog that is undergoing chemotherapy would be wise to eat gently cooked foods versus raw to avoid possible bacterial contamination. If raw is preferred, then extra caution should be taken to ensure that the food is made by a reputable manufacturer. Their immune system will be very delicate during treatment so extra precautions in all areas (i.e., what they eat, where they walk, and who they play with) are valid considerations. It is also not advised to supplement your dog with antioxidants during chemotherapy as it may negatively affect the outcome of those treatments.

In all cases, the recommendations for a dog being treated for or recovering from cancer is to feed a high protein, moderate fat, low carbohydrate diet. Carbohydrates convert to sugar which in turn feeds the increased metabolic needs of cancer cells. Alternatively, proteins and fats are more readily utilized by normal healthy cells. We typically recommend a 70/30 mix of organic meat to organic low starch, low sugar veggies (i. e. broccoli, zucchini, kale).

Below is a list of some of the more common antioxidants, herbs and supplements that are thought to support the immune system, build healthy cells and prolong remission times in dogs recovering from cancer.

- **Antioxidants (A,E,C & Selenium)**.
- **Vivo Animals ZeoComplete Recovery Complex**. Excellent combination of herbs to detoxify the body and support proper immune function. Contains: organic food grade zeolite, organic reishi, organic cordyceps, wildcrafted mangosteen, vitamin C, glutathione, quercetin, alpha lipoic acid, organic seabed minerals, polycilfulvic / humic acid, organic chestnut seed extract, organic cinnamon, organic turmeric, organic raw cane sugar, aquamin, algae extract, and wildcrafted papaya.
- **Red Clover**. Restricts blood flow to tumors and cleanses the blood.
- **Organic Greens Supplement**. The phyto-nutrients found in green foods are full of vital anti-oxidants and plant-based vitamins and minerals. Green leafy foods increase the alkalinity of the body resulting in a lower inflammatory response. Many include an array of beneficial bacteria (probiotics), fructo-oligosacaccharides (prebiotics) and digestive enzymes.
- **CoQ10**. Immune support.
- **Dandelion**. Used to support digestion, liver function and as an anti-inflammatory.

- **Garlic**. In small daily doses, garlic can be used at a health tonic to support proper cellular metabolism. Also used as a natural antibacterial/antifungal.

- **L-Arginine**. Has shown to increase remission duration times in some types of cancer .

- **Cystine and Glutamine**. Amino acids that support the immune system.

- **Omega 3 Fatty Acids**. Transports fat soluble vitamins to cells to help support healthy cell growth.

- **Echinacea**. Immune support.

- **Astragalus**. Antiviral immune booster.

- **Cat's Claw**. Anti-tumor properties for cancers of the nervous system and brain.

- **Pau D Arco**. Anti cancer and anti-inflammatory.

- **Milk Thistle**. Supports the liver during chemotherapy.

- **Shark Cartilage**. Restricts blood flow to tumors.

Cure

I sincerely hope that one day in my life time I can look back at cancer as a thing of the past in both humans and dogs. At times, I feel that we are so close and yet I am constantly reminded of the other contributing factors that must come into alignment in order to make this hope a reality. Awareness really is the key. We can frown on puppy breeding mills and commercial pet foods but unless we make it our business to really understand the concerns behind these practices we are likely to inadvertently support them. We can live in fear of disease or we can take charge of what we put into our bodies and the bodies of our family members. Learn all you can and tell your friends. Support your local farmers by buying organic and sustainably raised foods. Learn to make your dog's food or find someone reputable that will. Learn to read labels. Research your dogs breed so that you can understand what cancer risks may be predominate in that breed. Quit spaying and neutering immature animals. Stop applying chemicals to your yards where your dogs and children play. Donate money to research a cure.

Massage Plans

In this section, I will show you the massage routine that I used with my dogs, as well as describe a few simple techniques by Megan Ayrault, a professional animal massage therapist. Megan's site, called www.AllAboutAnimalMassage.com, contains a wealth of information on animal massage, provided through free webinars and e-books.

According to Megan, there are many benefits to animal massage, including:

- Assists the nervous system to go into "relaxation mode" which is important because healing occurs when the body is relaxed, not when it is stressed.
- Strengthens immune system.
- Creates a deeper bond with you.
- Instills greater confidence
- Enhances communication so you can tell how they're feeling.

In addition, the following areas all experience benefit from massage: muscles; nerves; respiratory system; circulatory system; lymphatic system; skin; etc.

Simple Massage Routine

At the start of our simple massage routine, I would lower my head so that we were nose to nose, and I would tell him how much I loved him and that I was going to do a massage. Then, I would run my hands over his whole body from head to tail in long strokes (see pictures that follow). My purpose in doing so was to relax him and let him know that the massage was going to begin.

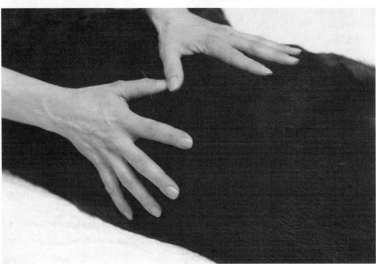

Then, I would slowly work over his whole body, massaging in this order:

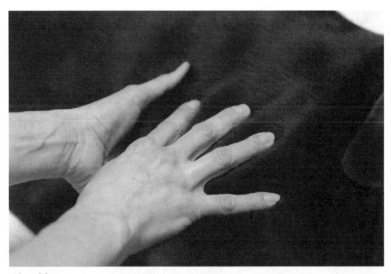

Shoulders

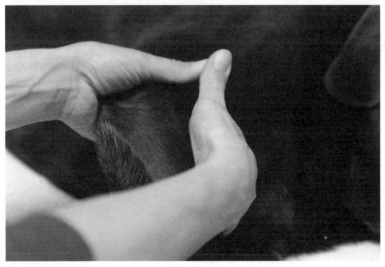

Arms, paws

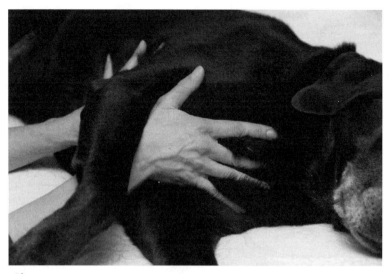

Chest

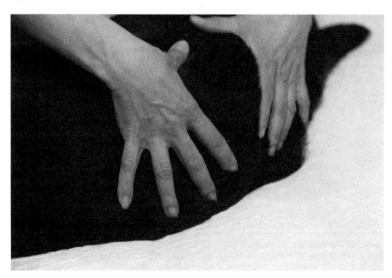

Back

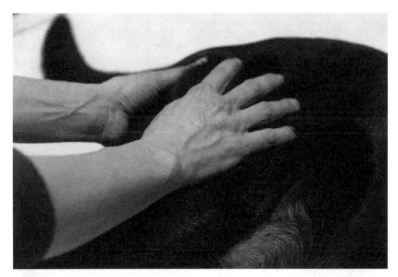

Hips

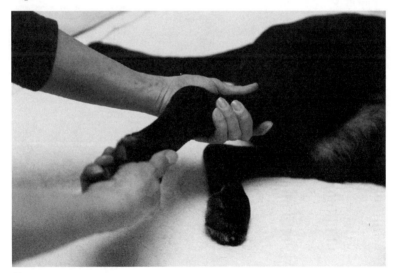

Legs, paws

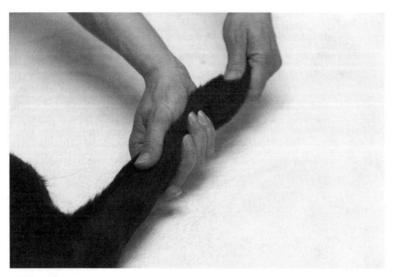

Tail

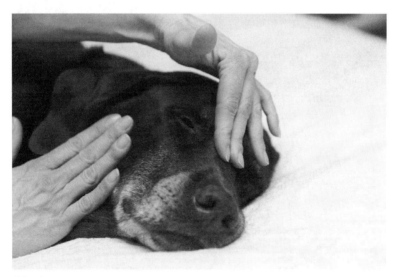

Head

The technique that I used was a gentle rubbing, to relieve any tension that was present and provide comfort to areas that were tender. I would finish with his head, massaging ears and face, ending nose to nose again. We'd look into each other's eyes for minutes on end, and it seemed almost that he could sense what was coming. True to his nature, he lived in the present and was able to enjoy every minute regardless.

Detailed Massage Plan

Megan stresses that your breath and visualization while you are administering the massage are key elements of how the massage session will be received by your dog. Maintaining a relaxed, deep breath while thinking positive thoughts will bring focus to the massage. Your stroke will become more deliberate and your intention will become clear. This will help focus your animal as well and enhance the healing process. She recommends a seven-step routine:

Step 1. Plan for Success

- Establish a routine time and place when your dog is calm.

Step 2. Breathe: Focus and Calm Your Energy

- Take deep breaths to focus your mind and prepare you for the massage.

Step 3. Visualize the Positive Results

- Visualize how calm and happy your dog will be after the massage.

Step 4. Say Hello with Your Hands – conscious beginning

- Gently touch your dog's shoulder with each hand; you can use the back of your hand if that is more calming.

Step 5. The Calm Down Points

- As your dog is sitting, place one hand on the shoulder, and the other on the chest; find the soft hollow spots in the chest, near the sternum.
- Use flat fingers and massage in small circles.
- Don't use fingertips or pressure.
- This triggers a relaxation response, as it is near important acupressure points for calming.
- To achieve lymphatic draining, use short strokes instead.

- See the following picture; my dog model, Scooby, was not comfortable sitting on the bed, so I improvised and modified the massage for a position lying down. It can be done either way.

Calm Down Points in a Lying Down Position.

Step 6. Balancing the Back

- This is a long stroke, all the way from your dog's head, along each side of the spine, to the tail.

- Another option is to continue over the back leg to the paw.

- A third option is to start from the forehead or inside edge of the eyes after the initial stroke.

- This works both the central nervous system and the Master (Bladder) Meridian of Eastern Medicine.

- To be effective, you must perform the stroke three times on each side of the spine.

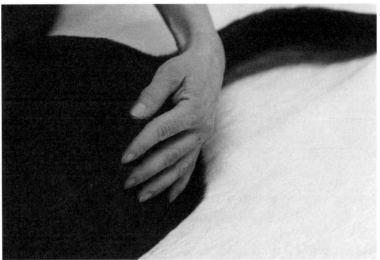

Balancing the Back on the right side of the spine towards the tail.

Step 7. Power Blessing

- End with deep breaths and both hands on your dog's body.

- Send positive thoughts and images to your dog.

When you first introduce massage to your dog, you cannot predict how he may respond. That is why it is important to be as calm and focused as possible when you initiate the massage. My dogs responded very well to massage; in fact, they enjoyed it so much, they would settle right in and lie down as soon as they realized what was about to happen. Anything you can accomplish for your dog with respect to massage will be beneficial to him. Don't be surprised that very powerful healing can occur even with one session.

Information on Pet Loss and Grief Support Lines

The list below was compiled at the time this book was published; it may be wise to do your own search to ensure that your results are most current:

University of Tennessee College of Veterinary Medicine

- www.vet.utk.edu/socialwork
- Services: Help Line, Message Line
- Phone: 865-755-8839
- Hours: Monday–Friday , 9 am–6 pm EST
- Notes: staffed by social work professionals. Initial calls are targeted for 20 minutes, but four free, one-hour individual grief counseling sessions are offered via phone.

College of Veterinary Medicine, Cornell University

- www.vet.cornell.edu/Org/Petloss/
- Services: Pet Loss Support Hotline
- Phone: 607-253-3932
- Hours: Tuesday–Thursday, 6–9 pm ET
- Notes: This is a very busy line; I was not able to get through.

The Iams Pet Loss Support Center & Hotline

- www.iams.com/pet-health/dog-article/the-death-of-a-pet
- Services: Support Line
- Phone: 888-332-7738
- Hours: Friday, 8 am–5 pm, ET
- Notes: A small team of customer relations staff. No limit to number or duration of calls.

Dove Lewis Emergency Animal Hospital Pet Loss Support Services

- www.dovelewis.org
- Services: 24-hr Message Line, Support group
- Phone: 503-234-2061
- Hours: 24 hours
- Notes: Support groups in Portland, OR four times a month. Free memorial arts therapy every second Sunday.

St. Hubert's Animal Welfare/Adoption Agency

- www.sthuberts.org
- Services: Support group
- Phone: 973-377-7094
- Notes: Support groups in Madison, NJ, first and third Tuesdays, staffed by two professional counselors.

College of Veterinary Medicine at the University of Illinois

- http://vetmed.illinois.edu/
- Services: Pet Loss Hotline, 24-hr Message Line
- Phone: 877-394-CARE (2273)
- Hours: Tuesday, Thursday, Sunday: 7–9 pm ET

The Animal Medical Center

- www.amcny.org
- Services: Support group
- Phone: 212-838-8100
- Notes: Support groups in New York, NY, every other Tuesday run by a licensed social worker.

Chicago Illinois VMA

- www.chicagovma.org/petlosssupport
- Services: Support Hotline, 24-hr Message Line, Support Group
- Phone: 630-325-1600
- Notes: Calls will be returned weekday evenings, 7–9 pm CT. Long distance calls will be returned collect. Support groups meet at 7:30 pm on the first Wednesday of the month in Burr Ridge.

University of Florida, Small Animal Hospital, College of Veterinary Medicine

- http://smallanimal.vethospital.ufl.edu/client-services/pet-loss-support/
- Services: Support Hotline, 24-hr Message Line
- Phone: 352-294-4430
- Notes: Calls returned within 24 hours on weekdays; weekend calls returned on Mondays.

Michigan State University School of Veterinary Medicine

- http://cvm.msu.edu/Plone/alumni-friends/information-for-animal-owners/pet-loss-support
- Services: Pet Loss Support Hotline, 24-hr Message Line
- Phone: 517-432-2696
- Hours: Tuesday–Thursday: 6:30–9:30 pm ET
- Notes: Support group in East Lansing, MI twice monthly; call for dates.

Tufts University School of Veterinary Medicine Pet Loss Support Hotline

- www.tufts.edu/vet/petloss/
- Services: Support Hotline, 24-hr Message Line, Internet Support Groups and Chat Rooms
- Phone: 508-839-7966
- Hours: Monday–Friday: 6–9 pm ET
- Notes: Visit their website for a list of internet support groups.

The Virginia-Maryland Regional College of Veterinary Medicine

- https://scholar.vt.edu/portal (you'll need to call to be provided with a username and password to access their site)
- Services: Support Hotline
- Phone: 540-231-8038
- Hours: Tuesday and Thursday: 6–9 pm ET
- Notes: Calls are limited to 30 minutes, but there is no limit to the number of calls that can be made. Counseling referrals are provided.

Washington State University, College of Veterinary Medicine, Pet Loss Partnership

- www.vetmed.wsu.edu/PLHL/
- Services: Support Hotline, 24-hr Message Line
- Phone: 866-266-8635 or 509-335-5704
- Hours: Monday, Wednesday, Thursday: 6:30–9 pm and Saturday 1–3 pm PT

University of Illinois College of Veterinary Medicine

- http://vetmed.illinois.edu/CARE/
- Phone: 877-394-2273
- Hours: Sunday, Tuesday and Thursday: 7–9 pm CT
- Notes: Each call has an hour limit, but you are welcome to call back as many times as you need.

Association for Pet Loss and Bereavement (APLB)

- www.aplb.org
- Services: Pet loss chat rooms available Monday, Tuesday, Wednesday and Friday from 8–10 PM ET; Sunday 2–4 PM ET; Thursday 7–9 PM ET. Anticipatory bereavement chat room available 1st and 3rd Thursdays, 8–10 PM ET.
- Notes: All chat rooms are moderated by trained pet loss counselors. All staff have completed APLB's pet loss counselor certification as well as an internship in the program. There are no restrictions regarding how often people may participate. This may be a good option for people who are more comfortable expressing their grief from the privacy of their own home.

ABOUT THE AUTHOR

Author Lola Ball her son, Connor Ball, and their dogs, Scooby Doo and Apollo in a grove of aspens in Guffey, Colorado, where they just spread Porter and Jasper's ashes.

Lola has been an avid animal lover since she was a little girl, but wasn't allowed to have a pet as a child due to family allergies. Once she was settled in her late 20's, she bonded quickly with her first puppy, a chocolate lab named Porter. It was when Porter was diagnosed with hemangiosarcoma that Lola inadvertently employed hospice care to ensure that his last few months would be of a high quality of life. After his death, she decided to capture her experiences with caring for a cancer dog by writing a book to share what she had learned, so that others would not have to start from ground zero. During the writing of this book, Jasper, a yellow lab-hound dog mix she adopted, was diagnosed with mast cell tumor and she again used hospice techniques on the path to a natural death. Her undergraduate days at MIT and a position at Los Alamos National Laboratory have grounded her in the ways of research, which has been an invaluable asset. She volunteers at Pasado's Safe Haven, where she enjoys being surrounded by dogs, cats and farm animals of all kinds! She is also an active volunteer in the local and national MIT Alumni Association. She currently serves as Secretary on the Board of Directors of the AHELP Project, based in Bellevue, WA and is an active volunteer with the international animal hospice organization, International Association of Animal Hospice and Palliative Care.

INDEX

A

Acetaminophen, 40
acupressure, 41, 44, 78, 81–82
acupuncture, 25, 30, 50, 81
adenocarcinoma, 119
age factors, 84
alfalfa, 66
All Pets Go To Heaven (Browne), 99
aloe vera, 66
alternative medicine. *See also* herbal medicine; holistic medicine
  caregiver team and, 12–13
  for pain relief, 43–45
amantadine, 40
American Kennel Club, 32
amitriptyline, 40
Animal Cancer Treatment Program, University of Wisconsin, 32
Animal Hospice, End-of-Life, and Palliative Care Project, The, 61, 74
antiangiogenic therapy, 24–25, 29
antihistamines, 46
antioxidants, 65–66, 69, 159
appetite, loss of
  coping with, 58–61
  as sign of cancer, 18, 88, 92
aspirate, needle, 10
astragalus, 66, 160
attitudes of caregivers, 77–78

B

Baked Beets recipe, 65
bathing, 77
Beets, Baked, 65
behaviors
  as indicator of cancer, 88
  as indicator of pain, 38
Bergman, P.J., 24, 74–75
biopsies for diagnosis, 10
Bittel, Ella, 4–5, 41, 54, 118
blindness, 18, 88, 121
blood analysis, 9
brachytherapy, 23

breed factors, 110, 114, 153, 158
brushing, 77
buprenorphine, 40
burdock, 67
burial, 96–97
butorphanol, 40

C

Calanni, Mary, 44, 80–81
cancer, types of, 14–19
cancer diagnosis, 8–13
cancer prevention, 82–89
cancer treatment plans. *See* treatments
Canine Health Foundation, 32
Canine Vaccination Protocol, 49
caregiver team, evaluation of, 12–13, 50
carprofen, 40
Castor Oil Wrap, 43–44
cat's claw, 66, 160
Cerenia, 16, 41
Chard, Sautéed, 65
chemotherapy
  massage and, 79–80
  nutrition and, 49–50, 55, 158–159
  overview, 22–23, 27
Chinese medicine. *See also* herbal medicine
  caregiver team and, 12
  herbs used, 70
  nutrition and, 86
  treatment plans, 25, 30
colostrum, 69
CoQ10, 159
costs of treatment, 32
coughing, 18, 88
counseling sessions, 100
cremation, 96–97
cryosurgery, 25, 29
curcumin, 69
Cystineand Glutamine, 160

D

dandelion, 68, 159
Death with Dignity Act, 5
degranulation events, 15–16
Deramaxx, 40–41
dercoxib, 40

Also available from Dogwise Publishing

Go to www.dogwise.com for more books and ebooks.

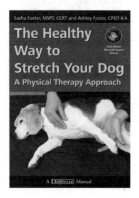

The Healthy Way to Stretch Your Dog
A Physical Therapy Approach
Sasha Foster, MSPT, CCRT and Ashley Foster, CPDT-KA

You have probably heard that humans need to stretch for good health. So do dogs. Now you can learn how to safely and effectively stretch your dog to prevent injuries, maintain joint integrity, and improve your dog's fitness, whether he is an elite canine athlete or a lap dog.

The Healthy Way to Stretch Your Dog
A Physical Therapy Approach with Activity Specific Stretching Routines DVD
Sasha Foster, MSPT, CCRT and Ashley Foster, CPDT-KA

This DVD demonstrates how to safely and effectively stretch each major muscle group. Teaches correct hand placement for joint stabilization and how to maintain good form. Stretching routines are presented for both large and small dogs, older dogs, and those that are involved in a variety of dog sports.

Unlocking the Canine Ancestral Diet
Healthier Dog Food the ABC Way
Steve Brown

Steve Brown, an expert on canine nutrition, shows how you can bring the benefits of the canine ancestral diet to your dog by feeding him differently as little as just one day a week. Follow Steve's ABCs to make improvements to whatever your dog currently eats.

Facing Farewell
Making the Decision to Euthanize Your Pet
Julie Reck, DVM

One of the most difficult aspects of being a pet owner is making end of life decisions for beloved dogs and cats. Author Julie Reck is a veterinarian who has devoted her professional career to helping owners make more informed decisions about euthanasia. In *Facing Farewell*, you will be provided with a complete description of the euthanasia procedure so that you will know what to expect and be confident that you have made the right choice for both you and your pet.

Canine Massage, 2nd Ed.
A Complete Reference Manual
Jean-Pierre Hourdebaigt, L.M.T.

Bring the well-known benefits of massage to your own dog or become a canine massage specialist. Over 100 illustrations and 100 photos, detailed examinations of muscular stress points, diagnoses, and treatments.

Dogwise.com your source for quality books, ebooks, DVDs, training tools and treats.

We've been selling to the dog fancier for more than 25 years and we carefully screen our products for quality information, safety, durability and FUN! You'll find something for every level of dog enthusiast on our website www.dogwise.com or drop by our store in Wenatchee, Washington.